"As if she's sitting right across from you chatting over hot tea (or coffee), and with courageous, soul-baring honesty, Jo Ann shares her story and the faith that ultimately mended her soul. Whether you need restoration or you're looking for a way to help others, Jo Ann gives you the resources to come away renewed. Encouraged. Inspired."

Nicole Notare, Editor, *Guideposts Magazine*

"This book was written just for me. Thank you for getting up every time you fell, for pushing through every time you felt you couldn't go a step further. You did it for me and I thank you. I honor the Christ in you, Who just didn't let you quit when you desperately wanted to! I am a fourty-seven-year-old Indian mom. I was born a Hindu, but received a great revelation of God's love for me, and am now Christian. In his Sovereignty, God made sure that I received a copy of your book. I now walk in a deeper level of freedom because of it. I thank you."

Rajes Reddy, Chief Operations Officer, Johannesburg, South Africa

"Jo Ann offers an honest, soul-deep exploration of the survivor in each of us. Based on faith and biblical lessons, this tightly-sculpted narrative will soothe scars and heal hearts of even the most broken spirits. This guide helps readers peel back our protective layers to remind us all that we are loved, that our lives have great purpose, and that the only path to freedom is through forgiveness and truth."

Julie Cantrell, New York Times and award-winning author of *Into the Free* and *When Mountains Move*

"*When A Woman Finds Her Voice* is such an important book for anyone who wants to mine the past, heal like crazy, and find joy today. Jo Ann Fore takes readers gently on a journey of discovery as she shares her own healing path with breathtaking authenticity. If you've wanted to live free from a painful past, pick up this book."

Mary DeMuth, author of *The Wall Around Your Heart*

"I read through *When A Woman Finds Her Voice* in one sitting. Jo Ann has a strong poetic voice that speaks to the hearts of women and calls them loved. Using her own story of abuse, alongside powerful anecdotes from others, Jo Ann offers comfort, prayers, and courage to those who've suffered in silence for far too long. An inspiring and moving read, and it is my hope that it will find a place on the shelves of every church and library in North America."

Emily T. Wierenga, author of *Chasing Silhouettes* and *Mom in the Mirror*

"There are words and sentences, lines and paragraphs so powerful within Jo Ann Fore's *When A Woman Finds Her Voice*, readers will be struck almost speechless by them. But then, within the Power behind them, new strength and a new voice will emerge. This is the beauty of the book . . . the awesomeness behind the writer and her God."

Eva Marie Everson, best-selling author of *Unconditional, the Novel*

"Jo Ann's story and use of Scripture as the way to heal and reclaim the right to speak one's truth is spiritually inspired. Her life experience, authentic voice, wisdom, and poetic narrative call you to remember your own struggles to speak your truth and to examine if there's more work to be done. I can't wait to share *When A Woman Finds Her Voice* with my patients, friends, and family. No matter their background and plight, I know this book will help to heal them."

Dr. Deborah M. Khoshaba, Founder of Psychology in Everyday Life

"Thank you Jo Ann for the transparency in your 'Voice'. This book, *When A Woman Finds Her Voice*, will resonate in the lives of many women who need to find their 'Voice' for healing and hope in the Lord. May this book bring freedom to the millions of women who need to speak up and speak out!"

Suellen Roberts, Founder & President of Christian Women in Media

"Have you been hurt so much that you can't tell anyone the details? Struggling to believe God could be real in the midst of your painful story? Jo Ann is the real deal. She shares real stories from her own life, along with the stories of others. Then she seamlessly weaves them with biblical truths, along with the healing remedies the very best counselors would offer."

Lucille Zimmerman, Licensed Professional Counselor/Affiliate Faculty Professor at Colorado Christian University; author of *Renewed: Finding Your Inner Happy in an Overwhelmed World*

"The healing words and gut-wrenching testimonies within the pages of *When A Woman Finds Her Voice* will rock your world. If you're serious about getting rid of those ugly wounds buried within the crevices of your heart, this amazing book is for you. With author Jo Ann Fore as your guide, you will be blessed."

Jan Coates, speaker, author of *Attitude-inize* and *Set Free*

"The title of this book is so very appropriate because Jo Ann has an amazing way with words. Her words both challenge and comfort, gently probe and encourage. After a lifetime of hearing lies and absorbing the shame of the behavior of others, those words are exactly what a hurting woman needs to hear. . . . This is a tremendous resource for beginning the recovery journey."

Dr. Morven R. Baker, PCC-S, NCC, Ashland Women's Counseling Center

"Jo Ann Fore's new book, *When A Woman Finds Her Voice*, is a sumptuous feast for a woman's wound-weary and fear-famished soul. After successfully using Jo Ann's journal, *Write Where It Hurts*, as a source of writing prompts for our ladies' journaling group last year, I am excited to embark on our group's new journey together as we trust the Lord to help us find our voices. Deeply moving and rich in wisdom, this book is saturated with truth and beauty from cover to cover, and will teach women how to unpack the pain, let in the Light, and learn to hear God's voice. Any women's bible study or ministry group needs this book."

Jo-Ann Sass, Women's Ministry Leader, Canada

"*When A Woman Finds Her Voice* is a powerful book full of honesty, understanding, and truth which will undoubtedly be a healing tool. The message of freedom through faith in Christ is refreshingly woven throughout; meanwhile, questions for reflection give readers an opportunity to go deeper in their healing—to not only find their voice, but to consider practical life skills that have the power to transform a broken life into a beautiful one."

Nicole Bromley, author of *Hush* and *Breathe*, Founder of OneVOICE

"JoAnn combines her gift of gentle storytelling with an unyielding passion for healing in this book which ultimately lets broken women know they are not alone. A powerful resource with practical tools that sojourners on the road toward healing will certainly return to, time and time again."

Amy K. Sorrells, award-winning author of *How Sweet the Sound*

"*When A Woman Finds Her Voice* drew me in immediately! Jo Ann's personal heartfelt testimony, powerful quotes, plus the telling of other women's true life stories are a powerful backdrop for this practical and inspiring piece of work. I love it because it combines story, faith-based words of wisdom and comfort, with practical exercises that will definitely help those who read it truly find their own voice. Thank you for writing a book that women from all walks of life have been waiting for! Let the healing begin."

Kelita Haverland, award-winning singer, songwriter, and justice advocate.

when a woman finds her Voice

Overcoming Life's Hurts & Using Your Story To Make A Difference

JO ANN FORE

When A Woman Finds Her Voice

Overcoming Life's Hurts & Using Your Story to Make A Difference

ISBN 978-0-89112-387-3

Printed in the United States of America

The Author is represented by and this book is published in association with the literary agency of WordServe Literary Group, Ltd., www.wordserveliterary.com.

Library of Congress Cataloging-in-Publication Data

Fore, Jo Ann, 1964-

When a woman finds her voice : how to live free from life's hurts / Jo Ann Fore.

pages cm

Includes bibliographical references.

ISBN 978-0-89112-387-3

1. Christian women--Religious life. 2. Interpersonal communication--Religious aspects--Christianity. 3. Silence--Religious aspects--Christianity. I. Title.

BV4527.F665 2013

248.8'43--dc23

2013024731

Interior text design by Becky Hawley

Cover design by Christine E. Dupre

Leafwood Publishers is an imprint of
Abilene Christian University Press
1626 Campus Court
Abilene, Texas 79601
1-877-816-4455
www.leafwoodpublishers.com

13 14 15 16 17 18 / 7 6 5 4 3 2 1

For the soul-wounded woman.

Your healed voice is my favorite sound.

Your hurts,

they walk right into our hearts;

but your story of healing—that can change lives.

Never be afraid to find and use your voice.

Contents

Foreword

Eons ago, before you were ever born, God designed you with a unique purpose to discover and fulfill on earth. He's always intended to use every part of your life—no matter how broken—in his Kingdom-building plan.

Jo Ann is just the right person to walk alongside you on this unparalleled adventure of finding your voice and unlocking your God-given purpose. She's walked this journey. She's also learned that regardless of how intensely you long to do something great for God, emotional wholeness is your top-priority purpose in life.

Do you struggle with the fallout of an emotionally painful experience? Have you been allowing fear, intimidation, or feelings of worthlessness to thwart your God-inspired "this-I-must-do" legacy? Maybe you've spent years as a people pleaser, performer, or perfectionist, allowing the expectations or caustic words of others to somehow control you.

Through timeless truths, Jo Ann guides you into a safe place to loose those chains and live out the destiny God is offering you. Under her direction, voicelessness loses its wicked grasp and no longer blocks the abundant life God wants you to live.

Every woman has a story, and far too many of those stories have left scars. As one of our certified coach-facilitators at Life Purpose Coaching Centers International®, Jo Ann gently and artfully draws out your story. And she dresses any hidden hurts with the bountiful hope that God is masterful at using this pain for good.

Your Creator has gifted you with a distinctive life–message to share with a specific group of people in a particular way. As you actively participate in *When A Woman Finds Her Voice*, you will uncover practical tools that empower you to respond to his invitation to carry that message to those he's sending you to serve. You'll find your voice!

—Katie Brazelton, PhD, MDiv, MA
Bestselling author, *Pathway to Purpose for Women*
Founder, Life Purpose Coaching Centers International®
Board Member, International Christian Coaching Association

Introduction

Only one thing is more frightening than speaking your truth,
and that is not speaking.
~Naomi Wolf

I blame Disney.

Those storybook tales we held to as we grew up—the wonder and magic of happy endings—oh how those dreams and expectations can set a girl up for disappointment when life gets hard.

And at some point, life always gets hard.

I remember the day I surrendered my happily-ever-after, that day I sat cross-legged on the bare hardwood of my living room, a thirty-something worn-out mama and abandoned wife. My fears, doubts, and insecurities sparkling much brighter than my trampled tiara.

Broken dreams and unmet expectations leave invisible wounds, ones that linger, confuse, and overwhelm. Our souls stained, our hearts wrecked, we tend to lose hope. Our mouths broken, we fall silent.

While silence can be serene and comforting when we need a break from daily living, silencing who we are, our internal voices, weakens our ability to connect heart-to-heart with others.

Over time, our voices can fade to insignificance. The nothingness permeates our lives with low self-esteem and threatens to steal our very identities.

Have you (or someone you know) ever fallen silent? Felt unable to express yourself because you were misunderstood, attacked, or criticized in some way? Have you ever hurt so badly you doubted the pain could go away? More importantly, have you felt a sharp pull to hide these hurts?

That's not God's plan.

Your voice matters. In fact, it's a personal gift from the One who made you.

Pull that truth in tight—to the very core of your being. Relish the freedom.

You aren't alone. Unworthy. Powerless. You are important in God's eyes. You aren't defined by what has happened to you, or even your own wrong choices; these things will not destroy you. You are loved. Needed. And what you have to say is valuable.

Intoxicating, isn't it?

Those thin places
where truth seeps through—
those are the places where Jesus walks,
the places we find healing.

Dare you believe it? The Pollyanna euphemisms can fade quickly as you default to what you know best. After a brief interlude of hope, your mind pulls back, pulverized by self-doubt. *Is what I have to say really meaningful or valued—does anyone even care?*

It's hard to forget those times you were forced to keep secrets. Or those times others made you feel worthless and inferior, pumping up their ego at the price of your self-worth.

This battle for our voices is intense. We want our freedoms. To feel joy. We want to matter. But our worlds are loud, filled with friends, family, and co-workers as well as social demands and outside negative influences.

And in the midst of all this noise, we tend to lose the voices that matter most—both our own and that of the God who whispers to our hearts.

I well know the roar of silence, the taste of fear. I've lived the numbing quiet of suppressed emotional pain caused by unfathomable hurts.

But I've also reached out and grasped the hand of freedom extended by a personal and loving God. I've come to savor the liberty to speak—to participate in my own life and the lives of those around me. No longer does life pass me by.

A tumultuous journey of childhood sexual abuse, a twenty-year struggle with bulimia, and emotional and physical abuse in a former "Christian" marriage threatened to derail God's purpose for my life. With a shattered sense of safety, I couldn't believe God, much less trust him. With a brain hardwired by destructive negativity, I made countless poor choices. And the fallout of those painful life experiences left me vulnerable. Voiceless for years.

But it didn't have to be that way.

Over time, in the healing shadow of Jesus, I addressed the toxic beliefs that had soiled my life and twisted my thinking. As I learned to identify these lies and replace them with truth, I couldn't help but think differently. Unaware, in the midst of it, I was retraining my brain.

The first step toward freedom is to choose truth.

Today, I use my formerly silenced voice to tell others about God's goodness and the plan he has for us to live a life of joy and purpose. A full life. A free life.

I don't share my story, or the stories of others, to sensationalize or compare. I'm gut-transparent about the cuts on my soul because I have benefited from the healing power that lies in this sort of exchange. Those times others have shared the messiness of their lives, those were the times I finally realized I wasn't alone. The times I found the courage to confront my own mess.

When we hear others say what we cannot,
we somehow start to make sense out of a pain
that can't otherwise be expressed.

I am one of many, only one out of countless women who have suffered hurts and wounds that slice soul-deep. Do I share this connection with you? While I don't know your story or situation, I do know that together we can gain strength to restore the lost years.

We can overcome these things that have hurt us and reclaim our voices, using them to make a difference.

That Unnerving Time We Approach a Crossroad

Even before we were born, there was hope for the power of our voices. It was assumed we would speak—important that we did. At birth, family members pressed in to ensure our lungs drew in bittersweet air. Unworried with thoughts or expectations of others, unencumbered by concerns of value, worth, or meaning, and in our most primal and authentic voice, we cried out. Signaled by the sound, everyone celebrated new life.

Somewhere along the way we lost that celebration of unimpaired voice. Many of us were shamed, intimidated, or bullied into a habit of silence. In time, we adopted a false voice; we put on a "life-is-just-fine, thanks-for-asking" mask while we lived a life on the outside that was deeply divorced from our innermost truth.

We isolated. We sat at home (at work, at church), adjusting our false faces. *Keep it in check. No one can know. No one will understand—they may even blame me. Now's not the time to crack.*

Meanwhile we did what "good Christian women" do: we buried ourselves in family, career, and service to others, pretending immunity from any past or present emotional wounds. Too often, we abandoned healthy boundaries at the first sign of resistance while we let the responsibilities of life postpone our dreams.

But we remain silenced at a high risk. When we're afraid of the power of others over us, we can never know the depth of God's love, the width of his plans.

In *When A Woman Finds Her Voice*, we meet, face-to-face, a hope strong enough to overcome life's hurts—a hope that challenges us, encouraging us to make some tough but important life-changing choices.

My heart in writing this book is to help you become a Silence-Breaker, a woman willing to find and use her voice.

That story you're scared to share—
that story has the power to change
both your life and the lives of others.

Are you ready to escape this prison of holding back, of living in fear? Are you willing to reclaim your stalled dreams? As I share with you how God set me free from many agonizing hurts, my story will lead you into a safe place, one where you confront your own pain. We were not meant to spend our lives avoiding pain; it's time to overcome these lingering hurts that are holding you back.

This journey requires a level of involvement. Our time together will be interactive, not magical. The pages that follow offer life skills and practical resources that will bring healing, if you're willing to do the work. This is something you're going to have to both believe and do.

When reading a book, we're often tempted to do the exercises mentally without setting aside a special time of reflection and application. If this book is handled in that manner, it will simply join the other well-meaning books in our collections—the ones that offer a temporary respite, a fleeting ray of light that fades with the coming of the next storm. So I encourage you now, grab your favorite journal or a simple spiral-bound notebook in order to fully participate.

True emotional healing lies somewhere
between intentional choices
and divine intervention,
a junction of surrender, faith, trust, and action.

Whether you need emotional healing or are looking for tools to help others, *When A Woman Finds Her Voice* offers practical hope, straight talk, and insightful biblical truths that lead you to find this healing, and then helps you lead others to do the same:

- Learn to identify lies (false voices) and replace them with truth.
- Pull down mental traps and strip away their sense of power.
- Connect within healthy community, even when you've been hurt.
- Tame your emotions and focus on what matters.
- Move beyond lingering hurts.
- Shake free from shame, isolation, and other faulty thinking.
- Make intentional choices that bring lasting change.
- Uncover and protect your life purpose.
- Share the stories you've been hesitant to share.

I've walked this path of silence. A difficult and complex maze it was, but I never walked alone. It was a hard gateway to God, but a traceable one. Through the journey, I uncovered my voice, my authentic self. Ironically, with each new step I found myself leaning into this already-existing place, an identity God fashioned long ago.

It wasn't the discovery process I imagined it would be—not an individual journey but rather one with a communal impact. Funny how when you start to believe your voice matters, it starts to matter, becomes a healing light in the darkest of places.

This is where healing begins. This moment, when you start to anticipate freedom. This heart-attitude of expectancy is the breeding ground for healed voices. God wants to do the same in your life that he has done (and continues to do) in mine. Will you believe that, be prepared for it when it comes?

The pages to come lead you to a frightening yet liberating crossroads, one that determines your future. Will you continue to allow the hurts of life to intimidate and control you? Or will you shift your focus to what God has planned; will you choose a life of freedom, joy, and purpose?

Before you decide, consider what God has to say about it: "Don't let anyone intimidate or silence you. No matter what happens, I'm with you."[1]

When Silence Fell

Why We Allow Fear and Hurt to Cloud Our Hope

A voice is a human gift; it should be cherished and used. . . .
Powerlessness and silence go together.
~Margaret Atwood

I inched my way down the long hall, afraid to exhale. As I turned my head to make certain no one saw me, my shoulder brushed the cheap reproduction of the *Creation of Adam* painting hanging on the wall. I froze. My eyes locked onto the exit door, a short five feet away from me.

I hope no one heard. I took a deep breath and another step forward.

"There you are." My co-worker, Karen Trigg, stepped into the hallway wearing a warm smile that wrapped through to her hazel eyes. "A few of us are heading out for lunch in a bit; want to join us?"

That's the last thing I want to do. I simply wanted to sneak out, grab something to eat without anyone noticing. I cannot believe I left my lunch at home—how stupid. I scolded myself silently—a habit that came all too easily.

"No, thanks." I shifted my eyes toward the door and fumbled for my keys. "My lunch is in the car—forgot to bring it in this morning."

A few weeks back, Karen had joined our office at the faith-based non-profit organization where I worked. Things were much easier before she came; the executive director deferred to my preference to be alone.

But then bubbly, I-have-a-perfect-life Karen showed up. Karen, who had a strong faith, a strong support system, and a strong marriage. Karen, who was making friends with everyone in record time.

The sun didn't shine quite so brightly for me. Life was hard. I was married to a real Jekyll and Hyde who was sweet and charming one day and emotionally and physically abusive the next. He would ask for forgiveness and I'd give in, wanting to believe he would change. And he would . . . but not for long. I was convinced the abuse would end—that we would heal and have a good Christian marriage. But lately I questioned if anything I believed could be trusted.

My skittish circle-making around Karen's repeat invitations continued. I dismissed her with a new excuse at every turn. Whatever it took—even if it was a lie.

As a peer, Karen was great. She was enthusiastic, detailed, punctual. Our joint projects ran smoothly; that was important to me. But those times she wanted to go deeper, that made me extremely uncomfortable.

One day, Karen stood in my office doorway. "I'm glad we were paired together on this new project. Wanna grab a cup of coffee after work? It would be nice to know each other better."

I'd rather run, hide.

I managed to conceal my anxiety and addressed her matter-of-factly. "Karen, I just don't have time for friendships." I tucked my head down, looking at my day planner, rubbing my hand over its open pages. I shifted uncomfortably in my rolling desk chair, hoping she would realize I wanted her to drop this whole connecting thing.

"Maybe there's something I can help you do? Something that would free your schedule?"

"Thank you," I said. "But this is stuff I have to do myself."

"If you change your mind, I'm right down the hall."

Don't I know it. And how I wish you weren't.

Words That Whisper from Within

Secretly, I envied women like Karen who were connectors. Women who had the fortunate knack of seeming to love everyone. Women with a stable husband and loving family. Women who seemed to connect with their husbands, their children, and, well, almost anyone with relative ease. And perhaps what I envied most about connecty women was that they weren't afraid to meet other women for lunch or coffee for fear of their secrets leaking out.

Karen could never understand what I'm going through, nor could anyone else. They would think it's my fault. I was embarrassed, ashamed.

What if someone finds out, questions my position in ministry? I was a professional, a woman who held the attention of board members, CEOs, and affluent donors at important meetings and fundraisers. I could never admit I was one of "those women"—battered wives whom others judged and whispered about, saying things like, "What's wrong with her? Why doesn't she just leave the jerk?"

My secret-guarding continued as I made countless excuses for why my family didn't join the after-work get-togethers, and why I had so many hushed phone conversations with my husband during the day.

Karen's obtrusive kindness and desire to connect ignited a familiar anxiety within me—I did not want to be "found out."

This protective silence fell early in life, claiming its role as my closest companion. At ten years old, I wasn't like the other kids. With my washed-out skin, freckle-blotched face, and reddish-orange hair, I was sometimes a target for the mean kids' jokes. Oh I had friends, but we were never part of the cool crowd. That alone left a girl vulnerable and insecure.

But I had differences that ran much deeper than any physical appearance or social cliques. I harbored some harrowing secrets about my father, and I was taught early on that you don't tell secrets. In time, I learned to fake a normalcy that hid the pain—a normalcy I would never feel.

For years silence was my willing guardian, shielding me from the shame of an abusive father, the disgrace of revealing family secrets, and the pain of low self-worth. And now, with Karen pressing in, silence was once again my natural and welcome default—the familiar pain suppressing my heart.

There's something that happens
when silence hangs like shadows,
when brokenness stains the spirit,
when the lining of hope sheds from the heart.

The painful after effects of emotional wounds permeate our souls, negatively impacting the choices we make and the way we live. The longer we push aside these wounds, the greater the chance they will become contaminated. Infected. These wounds then weep, leaking and spreading into other areas, requiring additional care and taking much longer to heal. Gone unchecked, these infections often become much worse than the original wound.

I wonder if you have a weeping wound, an area in your life that is still contaminated.

Stepping into Our Scars

Life leaves scars—we all have our stories.

But scars shouldn't hurt, shouldn't be a fresh pain. Properly healed scars are closed, insensitive to touch. A faint reminder of something that once was. I have places on my body from bike wrecks, surgeries, and maybe even a dog bite, but those wounds are healed, closed off by scars. Not too long ago though, I had an open wound on my body and when I touched it, it hurt like mad. I was obnoxiously overprotective of this sore spot, not allowing anyone near for fear they would bump me.

I wonder how many of us are living in fear of being bumped.

If there is something in the recesses of our minds (those places we don't let others see) that shoots pain when it is "touched," we are still wounded. Our relationships infected. The best way to clean a wound like this is to properly flush it out.

Nature could tutor us in this area, this healing of hurts. In his book *Waking the Tiger*, therapist and educator Dr. Peter Levine suggests we could learn a valuable lesson from the instinctive behavior of animals. Those in the wild apparently hold an uncanny ability to process and transform traumatic life experiences.

In his studies, Dr. Levine noticed how most animals experience physical tremors after surviving a near-death pursuit. Once they escaped becoming someone's dinner, they ran around, shook, cried aloud—whatever it took to release the enormous amount of negatively charged emotions that had overpowered them during the chase.

There is a healing power that lies in the release of bound emotions.

Contrary to what we've heard, this licking our wounds is not always a self-pity thing. Before we can find healing, a gradual, intentional release of energy must take place. It is appropriate, necessary, to give ourselves room to address emotional pain so that we can heal and move forward.

If for some reason an animal failed to process his compressed energy, and tried to return to regular life still hyped up, he simply couldn't survive. If he didn't do this release-dance, these fragments of trauma eventually destroyed his ability to live a normal life.

Dr. Levine suggests we are much the same.

Repressed anxiety affects our attitudes, shapes our lives.

"There has to be a mechanism that's there to bring us back from the brink of insanity, the brink of fear and experience of threat to balance," Dr. Levine writes. "A threatened human must discharge all the energy mobilized . . . this residual energy does not simply go away."[2]

I have my days when I feel a little crazy myself, out of balance, fearful and hyped up. It's then that I know I've stuffed something, failed to process a hurt.

If we stuff these emotions long enough, our hearts eventually line up with the lie that we have to keep this pain hidden. God wants us to stop hiding our brokenness. Is there something you have been ignoring, hoping it will eventually go away?

> It's simply not possible to disconnect ourselves completely from those people and things which comprise our past just by salvation or the years between us. . . . They can still be affecting our attitudes, behaviors, personalities, fears, relational ability, health, or view of the world, and of God.[3]

Like adjusting a rearview mirror to eliminate some pesky blind spot, sometimes we have to take a look back (at our scars) to make sure there's nothing coming. No negative influences sneaking up on us that could cause a crash.

Those things we stuff, try so hard to ignore,
they are the very things begging for release
—the things that hold the promise of hope,
the flame of freedom.

Winning Best Dressed at the Masquerade Ball

"I was three when I bit my four-year-old stepsister for taking my tricycle," my friend Lisa Easterling recently shared. "My stepfather, Jim, came out of nowhere. He kept hitting me over and over; I didn't know if he was ever going to stop. I turned black and blue from the waist down and although my mother cried, she feared crossing him. I feared Jim more than I'd ever feared anything, and hated him even more than that."

The original lie, sewn by Jim but watered by Lisa's wounded thinking: "I dare not open my mouth in protest. Ever."

If any remnant of Lisa's voice remained after Jim's angry beating, it was soon wiped out. Starting at age six, another family member sexually abused Lisa for five years. *If you tell on me, they'll send me to jail—and that will upset everyone.* The lie of Lisa's abuser played repeatedly in her mind, frightening her and guilting her into silence. A lie that set the stage for a lifelong aversion to confrontation of any kind, the emotional paralysis lingering into Lisa's later years.

"Either I feared retaliation or I felt guilty for upsetting someone or getting them into trouble. My nurturing nature was twisted like a gun-barrel back into my face. Silence was safer and kept everyone happy—or at least not angry at me."

Manipulative fear often neutralizes the rational voice, rendering it ineffective.

This is why we so easily buy the lie that we should bury our hurts. This is why we withdraw, refuse to dialogue the pain. It's what we've been taught, these lessons that determine our life-attitudes.

This fatal falling for lies was modeled for us long ago in a beautiful garden where Eve was tricked, deceived.[4] Eve—the first woman, first wife, first mother, and the first one of us to fall for an ugly lie. That day Satan met Eve in the garden, he brought a convincing argument—one intended to lead her, and any of us who would follow, away from God's truth.

I mean, really—the woman was in a beautiful, perfect environment with the perfect man. I can't think of anything more satisfying than a clean house and a godly husband who loves you. Eve had both. And there wasn't another woman alive to compare herself with. *Heaven on earth.* Yet Satan found a way to convince her she deserved more. That somehow she didn't measure up and God was holding out on her.

Unfortunately, Eve's choice to believe that lie was one emotionally expensive lesson with some far-reaching consequences.

1. She fell right into Satan's plan.
2. She influenced someone else (Adam), who accepted a lie.
3. She rerouted God's plans for her and her family.
4. She gave in to fear.
5. She withdrew from God.
6. She blamed someone else for her mistakes.
7. She, and her family, suffered long-term emotional pain.

Oh, and let's not forget to update Eve's resume. In addition to her already impressive list of firsts (mom, wife, etc.), now Eve has become the first mask-maker, first actor. In accepting Satan's lie, she was forced to wear the lie, portray the character. Early on, she modeled for us girls how to "play the part."

Ah, the cancerous power of lies: shame and blame, deceit and manipulation, fear and control. A life lived outside of God's plan.

How many of us are doing the same thing? Cowering to fear, falling for lies?

Sometimes we cling to silence (no matter how terrible) simply because it's familiar. While miserable, life is at least predictable; and if we try to change, it may prove too painful, right? This is a lie; the same sort of lie that tripped Eve.

God's not holding out on us—his plan *is good*. We've got to learn to trust him and to stop playing the role Satan desires for us.

Let's consider some of our own mask-wearing behaviors, and the lies behind them that keep us trapped. Take a moment and read through these potential masks, marking each one you've either worn or been tempted to wear this week.

> **The People Pleaser**—I will do whatever it takes to make you happy, to keep the environment calm, safe, and stress-free. I will sacrifice my own needs in order to meet yours. When I do, you will love me.

> **The Approval Addict**—I need you to think highly of me, to always accept me. I will, at all costs, seek your approval. The more you validate me, the more I am motivated to pursue your praise.

> **The Performer**—I need to be productive. I cannot fail, especially in front of you. I often fake a super-competency I don't feel, because, after all, my worth is determined by my success.

The At-All-Costs Attractive—To gain your acceptance or love, I must be beautiful—or as close as I can get anyway. It is my duty. I must hide any flaws, imperfections, and anything that would not be pleasing to you.

The Perfectionist—I must stay in control. Do everything right. Regardless of the burden of responsibility I take on, I press forward. I won't ask you to help me, for I fear you won't be able to do it right. Yet, I crave your help. Your love. Your acceptance.

How elaborately we dance, pretending to be anyone but ourselves, spinning alongside others we think we know but really don't. Performing for acceptance, compromising for love. Always wondering if we're good enough, pretty enough, smart enough.

We're not-so-secret wrecks. We all know it, but we don't talk about it. Instead, we grab the mask that hides what we lack. And if that mask doesn't work, we mask our masks. Everyone does. We expect them to. If they stopped, we might have to.

We intend to hide our shortcomings
and the fear inside our hearts,
but instead, we hide our beauty, our true selves.

The View from behind the Mask

Lord, I prayed one morning driving to work, *I feel so cut off from everyone. Especially you. Don't you see what I'm going through? How can you not intervene? Can't you help me find a way out of this? I thought you were everywhere, could do anything—where are you now?*

Anger and confusion have often driven me right into Satan's plans, into his waiting arms where I believed his lie: *as I am, I am not enough*. In those times, I reach for my masks, decorate a new me that could adapt to most any environment.

No, really, things are okay. I can do this. Lots of people have it worse than me; this isn't so bad. I'm capable, confident. I'm a survivor. I don't need anyone.

False beliefs and soul-scars from my childhood had convinced me I could never measure up, but my masks promised otherwise. I *could* be that person others expected me to be. I could be calm and always happy. Meticulously put together. Syrupy sweet. Wildly successful without ever being afraid.

I learned to ignore the face behind these masks, the real live me, eventually, trading myself for a substitute. An artificial me that cared nothing about my dreams, about who I really was, was now running my life.

When wounds cut deep,
the opinions of others sometimes matters most.

If we aren't careful, we allow these triggered-by-others insecurities to rewrite our life stories, to shape our lives so negatively that we lose direction.

Consider again the impact that someone else's opinion had, not just on Eve, but on her husband. After the fruit-sharing, Adam was desperate to fix things—laying blame and excusing away his actions, "I was afraid . . . I was naked and I hid."

"Who told you that?" God asked.

I just love the question. God well knew the source of their shackling guilt, but I believe he wanted them to consider that someone else, a shrewd and conniving enemy, had influenced their beliefs.

The winds of accountability fell fresh among the trees in the garden that night.

That same wind is stirring now as God asks us the same thing: "Who told you that?" Who has lied to us? Diminished or ignored our true worth? Patronized or belittled us?

Who told you that you are worthless?
Not good enough? Unlovable?
That what you say doesn't matter?

What life-messages are we responding to? Criticism from a cynical "friend"? A family-imposed silence? Shame from an abusive spouse? Close relationships with narcissists, know-it-alls, controlling or belittling people? A toxic religious system, even?

No matter the messenger, we must wrest ourselves from these grips of shame and fear that keep us from truth. We must remind ourselves what God thinks about us. Do these messages line up with what God says about who we are?

Christian author and speaker Mary DeMuth is one who has had lies of worthlessness whispered to her soul: "You're dirty. Alone. No one loves you."

When she was only five, Mary was repeatedly raped by two neighborhood boys. A monopolizing fear followed her into adult life, holding her hostage for years. Most nights, instead of sleeping, she imagined horrific things happening to her.

> *Growing up, I had a monster-like fear of death. At night, I shivered as I prayed prayers to ward off ghosts.*
>
> *I avoided intimacy as much as I could so I wouldn't rip open a festering wound I couldn't handle. But you need to be willing to "go there" with Jesus. So many people aren't healed because they are afraid to open up the can of worms of their past. I'm here to say, yes it will hurt, but that kind of hurt is what heals.*
>
> *We'll never drink from the forest's mountain spring if we don't go through the tunnel. But most of us feel too afraid to step inside for fear of the dark; and the barren land—bleak as it is—has a staid familiarity about it. The truth? It's dark in the tunnel. The hurt is intensified, especially when we can't see the other side.*[5]

Emotionally isolated and relationally inept, Mary walked many painful years in repressive denial—until she was willing to accept truth. Facing the truth changed her heart. Her mind. Her life.

> *The healing came when I chose to no longer be silent. When I decided it was time to tell my story, ask for prayer, and trust God to heal me. A life of secrets seldom heals.*

There are those times we're afraid of the dark,
but our fears don't mean there is actually danger.
God is in the darkness with us, and he can see.
His very presence illuminates the dark,
driving it out.

When One Lie Is Not Enough

When Satan asked Eve, "Did God really say . . . ," he was laying a foundation of doubt, something he could build on. As Satan whispered discouraging deceptions, Eve's confidence weakened; she started questioning her ability to hear and understand God.

With only four words, Satan ripped a gaping hole in the first woman's relationship with her Creator, and he's been reopening that same wound in our hearts ever since.

If Eve, tucked away in the realms of paradise, can be deceived, consider how much easier it is for those of us walking out ordinary, everyday lives.

Satan uses life's hurts. From our wounds, he fashions a manipulative lie and wraps it securely around our hearts (the core of our souls). These lies grow invisibly in our root systems until they are imbedded, planted as truth. They shape our beliefs and personalities, dictating our behaviors, training us to act, or react, in certain ways. If we are still controlled by the fallout of a particular event in our lives, chances are we never reached the bottom layer—the core lie from which everything is shaped.

I'm a recovering perfectionist. This pursuit of perfection, a fruitless journey to somehow prove my worth. You see, my core lie is that I'm not good enough. I often drive myself (and those around me) batty trying to be Ms. Super-Achiever, controlling things I have no business controlling. All because of unreasonably high standards I long ago placed on myself.

While excellence is a respected virtue, it's more than that with me. Those times I don't have it all together, I sure want you to think I do. It's actually painful for me to fail in front of you. When I fail, my belief system tells me, "You see, you *aren't* good enough!"

The lies we believe stand behind every negative thought percolating in our minds. These beliefs limit what we think we deserve because of who we think we are.

Emotional wounds have their own convincing language, and too often we make decisions based on the voices of those wounds. It's a survival code, a coping mechanism of sorts. For example, if someone we love betrays us, we may commit to never trust again. If someone rejects us, we decide we'll never fit in no matter how hard we try. We aren't always fully aware that we make these crippling covenants, but this is the sort of thing that happens when we allow our emotions to make our decisions.

Like weeds in a garden, Satan loves planting lies that choke out truth. And he's thrilled when the weeds bloom so cute that it's hard for us to tell the difference, hard to tell they are lies until they've already taken root.

I'm no gardener but I've learned the trick for getting rid of these pesky weeds. Start with soft soil; the softer the soil, the easier the process. Then, trace the roots back to where they first broke ground. From there, gently twist the weeds and pull upwards—but not so hard they snap. If you snap the weed without going to the root, it only eliminates them temporarily and we don't want these things growing back. You'll be left with a hole where the weed once was; ideally, you'll shake the excess dirt off the roots and use it to fill most of this hole. You may still see a slight dip, but time and care will eventually smooth the ground.

The truth of God's Word cuts through the
good and bad of our lives
like a trowel digging up hard-to-remove weeds
without damaging the plant.

Will we bring our hearts, tender and soft, ready to dig in? Will we ask God, "When did I first believe this lie?" And as he gently pulls the truth to the surface, will we give him room to grow within us, fill the void with his way of thinking?

Why Trusting Our Feelings Is Sometimes Dangerous

"Please, come away with me—bring your children with us." Becky Spencer's eyes met the plea of the songwriter she had worked closely with over the past months. Like a spike of water frozen in place, the words pierced her hungry heart. Becky had fallen in love and longed to run away.

There was a slight problem, though—her upcoming tenth wedding anniversary with her husband.

Various church projects had pitted a vulnerable Becky and her songwriter friend together. Conversations grew longer, deeper, and eventually intimate. Because of her love for God, she felt guilty, but the desire for this man was strong. Becky caved to the succulent feelings of validation and comfort, and soon found herself in an emotional affair. Unwilling to turn her back on God, she chose to remain in her marriage—but the choice infuriated her.

"God, you are a trickster—you duped me into marrying my husband. You don't care about my feelings," Becky said. "I'll still read my Bible, but I don't believe you will speak to me. Even if you do, I won't believe you."

God's truth dismantles a lie.
Strips away its false sense of power.

Have you ever wondered how life gets so messed up? While I don't discount that there are those hurts we have no control over, there are these times we *think* ourselves into a painful mess.

Character and mind-set follow the heart (our feelings); we shape our lives by our thoughts. Focusing on miserable things eventually makes us miserable, keeps us stuck in the hard places. But there is an alternative when this negativity threatens our hearts and minds. We can switch the focus. We can refuse to rehearse the negative and choose to reframe our lives with truth. There are entire books written on this subject so I'll keep my thoughts brief, and then we'll practice.

When I'm stuck, when I need to redirect my thoughts, I use a simple question: *Is there another way to think about this?*

Okay, now to practice. (Yes, it's that important.)

Let's consider some common faulty–thinking traps and reframe them with scriptures taken from *The Message* translation of the Bible.

Self-defeating thinking: When we default to automatic negative thoughts. When we sabotage the potential good.

- Mental trap: I simply can't change.
- Reframed thought: *When I fix my attention on God, I will be changed from the inside out* (Rom. 12:2).

Emotional reasoning: When our feelings dictate our situations—if we feel it, it must be true.

- Mental trap: I must deserve this.
- Reframed thought: *Through the grace of Jesus' sacrifice, I am worthy of love. Whoever hurts me hurts God, and that can't be good* (Zech. 2:8b).

Conclusion-jumping: Without facts to support our assumptions, we interpret things negatively and anticipate the worst.

- Mental trap: People will think I'm dumb; they will never listen to me.
- Reframed thought: *God himself gives me wisdom* (1 Cor. 1:30).

Overgeneralizations: When we think "always" and "never." We tend to consider one event as the catalyst to an ongoing, never-changing pattern.

- Mental trap: I can never say anything right; I may as well not ever speak up.
- Reframed thought: *God will give me the words and wisdom that will reduce my accusers to stammers and stutters* (Luke 21:15).

All-or-nothing thinking: When we think in extremes, view everything as black or white, good or bad—no gray areas. The times a simple setback seems a complete failure.

- Mental trap: I messed up again; I may as well give up.
- Reframed thought: *I may not have it together, but I am well on my way. . . . God is beckoning me forward. I'm off and running and not turning back* (Phil. 3:13–14).

Please don't write this exercise off as inspiring rote, another good-girl "to-do." No matter how messy your life is at the moment, this *is* your kickoff to emotional wholeness.

We won't break free from these lies until we learn to reframe them with truth *in the midst of the mess.*

In spite of her feelings, Becky made a powerful choice: she maintained communication with God.

"That (connection) allowed me to process the pain and find answers, much like a new mother who eats properly and takes her vitamins. As a mother processes the food, she provides nourishment for her own health and her suckling baby," Becky said. "My wounds became a window to my soul, then a door of invitation for God to move.

"God gave me promises for my marriage. And, he showed me how we can be taught, as women, to love our husbands. I didn't know that could be taught. I thought you either did or didn't love your husband and that was that.

"God instructed me to do for my husband the things I wanted to do for the other man I'd fallen in love with. Honestly, it made me sick to my stomach. But God blessed my obedience. My feelings toward my husband changed; I eventually fell in love with him—and learned that God had my best interest at heart all along."

God is greater than our feelings,
more powerful than our wandering minds
and insecure hearts.

Conditioning Ourselves for an Optimal Life

One day, I sat in my brooding spot—the wingback chair facing the forested area that lined the back of my house. The chair was tucked into the one dark corner of my living room and was just tall enough and stiff enough to keep me from loosening up and relaxing down into it. Perfect for reciting to God, slowly and self-righteously, all the hard stuff.

This is what I get, God? This "doing the right thing" is harder than you make it out to be, this is what I get for trying? Weren't the abuse and abandonment enough—now an illness that's gonna take me out? Really, God?

Over the years, I've noticed a surprising link in the numbers of women who have been emotionally wounded who also suffer with a chronic illness.

That equation includes me. A war between lies and truth led me to the ultimate battle for not just my emotional health, but also my physical well-being. My life had twisted out of control like some tornado-ravaged Midwestern town. A chronic illness was mocking me—robbing me of normalcy, threatening my relationships, and poisoning my goals.

After some time passed sitting in that chair, I halfheartedly leaned over and lifted a magazine from the wicker basket beside me. I started flipping through the latest copy of *Back to the Garden*, a health and nutrition magazine. *I can always dream of good health, right?*

But this one article caught my eyes. The author, Bill Irwin, practiced his profession as a certified counselor by merging a former discipline of clinical chemistry with counseling skills, and then covered it all under his faith in God.

In the feature, Bill explained how most health issues are directly linked with a nonsatisfying personal relationship, the stress of that relationship apparently serving as a negative influence on our immune systems.[6] But Bill suggested that can be reversed. That we have considerably more control than we realize over the way we act and think, and that our total outlook directly impacts our health.

"When we choose to think differently, think positive thoughts, our body responds positively," Bill wrote.

I sunk deep into my chair in spite of my resolved annoyance. *We can choose to think differently? And that choice impacts our health?* Although it sounded a little too good to me, a few days later, I contacted Bill to further examine his theory. Luckily, he agreed to chat.

"The body has a unique ability to heal itself from most anything, provided we line it up under God's mandated balance," Bill said. "We must bring all the elements of our basic needs into balance—the body, mind, psyche, and spirit."

> *How much are we sacrificing with our out-of-balance lives? The fatigue, pain, and frustration—are they strong enough motivators for us to consider real change?*

"You have to make intentional choices," Bill said. "The type of choices that bring your life into balance spiritually, physically, emotionally, and mentally. It's going to take discipline. But if you can learn to hold to the promises of Scripture and make certain behavioral changes, you will effectively take control of your life."

> *Living like we matter is an intentional step,*
> *one that gets us where we need to be.*

For years, my thinking was distorted. I wanted to change, but how? A hand of hope grabbed my heart—here was my *how.* Bill would help me. Bill, who was faith-filled, passionate, inspiring.

And blind.

Yes, God sent a blind man to help me see. Made sense, really, when you consider my own blind spots; unruly, raw-to-the-core emotions that ravaged any budding hope of emotional wholeness.

If Bill didn't use blindness as an excuse, how could I?

How Right–Thinking Fuels Our Dreams

Although dependent on others, Bill enjoyed a unique level of freedom most of us merely dream of. He was the only blind person to ever thru-hike the 2,168 miles of the Appalachian Trail.

Blindness wasn't Bill's first taste of a handicap, though. Alcoholism, loneliness, and childhood abuse haunted his earlier years. But his life was radically altered when he learned to tame his emotions and control his thoughts.

"It's not our external circumstances that dictate our quality of life, but rather our response to those circumstances," Bill said.

Every day we have a choice,
and the choices we make dictate our future.
Will we focus on our weaknesses, powerlessness,
or will we look for opportunities
to implement and experience change?

Bill's words wrapped fresh hope around a painfully raw heart. For years, my mind was bent toward self-defeating thoughts and behaviors. To think I was somehow contributing to that unhappiness? Imagine—a chosen misery. How does one respond to news like that?

I won't patronize. (I wouldn't dare.) Escaping negatively charged, emotionally disruptive memories is hard. All firsts are hard. But how bad do you want this—this life of fullness that God has designed?

For me, a former control freak and type-A overachiever, it was difficult to accept that emotional healing was not some task-driven process. That I couldn't just check this one off my list as I completed the necessary steps. But I *could* make better choices. And if God's essential truths governed those choices, I *would* walk in the freedom and joy I had long craved.

I understand how hard it is to face life's hurts, to feel such pain, and then to have someone encourage you to move beyond it. You may feel disloyal, as if you're lessening what happened somehow. I'm not asking you to discount the original hurt—I want you neither immune to it nor hardened by it. I'm asking you to go all the way through it. To no longer be afraid of it.

If you promise me you won't ignore the pain, I promise you I won't ask you to dismiss it. Together, we will honor it, identifying any part of it that Satan may be using to keep you trapped.

Remember, I'm sharing my story and the stories of others to offer you credentials. A resume of sorts. We get it—we've been there. I spent years at the mercy of negative emotions and wrong choices. But emotions can heal if we give them voice. Any freedom I experience in my life comes only because I intentionally choose to allow God's love and his truths to shape me. I trust that so much, I want the same for you.

Seeking God

God, are you there? I imagine we should talk.

There are these words that sit lodged in my throat, clutching at my heart, begging for release. This pain, it's always on the verge of speaking, even when I try to silence it. These hopes and dreams for my future, I can remember them even now, though life has tried its best to stamp them out.

But I'm afraid, Lord.

It's easier to be what I "should be," say what I "should say," hide away, lying to myself and trusting wrong feelings.

But this avoidance simply stirs a greater anxiety within my heart. I need your help. I'm desperate for your intervention, your healing. I want to be that woman, the one who made it through to the other side of the craziness in her life. The one who, yes, may have been hurt, but because you reworked her heart she stands whole. Emotionally whole. Free.

I don't understand these things that have happened in my life. How do I trust you—fully trust you, the way you ask—with this lingering confusion?

I need you to walk with me, to fight for me.

Help me to gently probe these deep pockets of pain that remain. Not so I can linger in the pain of the scars, but so that I can identify any negative behaviors that are blocking me from the freedom you designed for me to live in. Help me to stop living my life based on my feelings. To replace lies with truth.

I commit this healing journey to you. With you leading, I will walk it. Please bring me out of the other side free. Whole. Safe, validated, and respected. Please give my life meaning.

Thank you, Lord, for the work you are about to do in me.

With an open heart I pray. Amen.

THE VOICE STUDIO:

Responding to God's Call to Develop Our Voices

Recognizing the Powerlessness of Silence

1. Have you ever felt forced to keep a secret? Intimidated or shamed into keeping something quiet? What was it? How does it make you feel to write it out now? Does that secret filter into your daily life—the way you see things, choices you make?

2. How do you handle shame? And what do you do when you feel powerless to change?

3. Do you ever feel like you should "be over this by now"? If so, why do you think you aren't over it? Is the push to be "over this" external (coming from someone else) or

internal (coming from within yourself)? What is your response to this idea?

4. Did you recognize yourself in any of the masks—the people pleaser, perfectionist, or others? How do these masks seem to help you cope with any lingering pain?

5. What mental traps are you aware of? What action steps can you take to overcome those?

6. Have you made any sort of covenant with yourself? Never to trust? Never to love again? What lie triggered that response?

7. What is your most common default thinking pattern? Example: *There's no need to try to change.* Do you feel like that thought pattern is in line with God's Word? Why or why not?

8. What boundaries would you put into place if you felt like you could?

9. Are you ready to go beyond a routine relationship with God into a genuine healing experience? Can you think of some ways you could prepare yourself for this journey?

10. Why does your voice matter? Locate and memorize one scripture verse that reminds you of the importance of using your voice for God.

    Here is an example, but please also seek others, as it helps to personalize your healing journey. "Pray that I'll know what to say and have the courage to say it at the right time, telling the mystery to one and all, the Message that I . . . am responsible for getting out" (Eph. 6:19–20).

2

Outside the Garden

Connecting with Others, Even When We've Been Hurt

To experience the joy of connection is life;
to not experience it is death to our souls,
death to our deepest desires,
death to everything that makes us human.
~Larry Crabb

"Just do what I tell you and I won't hurt you."

The sun bore down on my seven-year-old face. I lay beneath a massive pine tree, staring at the sky. Unguarded, I trusted him.

His eyes turned dark. His thick brows knitted together while an unfamiliar look contorted his face.

"Don't ever tell anyone," he said when he was finished. "Something really bad will happen if you do." Salty tears watered the dry, bitter nausea rising in my throat. My neck grew taut and intense heat swept across my cheeks. My heart pounded in fear.

Had I done something wrong?

He lied. He did hurt me. Cruelly and selfishly he violated me, betraying and shattering my innocence.

Is this what fathers do?

In my early years, my father abused me more times than I can recall. Inherently, I knew something wasn't right, but his threats attacked my sense of normalcy—convinced me no one would believe, or even care.

How do I tell the secret? Make him stop? Trapped in fear, I felt powerless. Shamed into silence. My father was a formidable man. Black-hearted, intimidating, and dangerous.

How does a child rationalize such pain?

Stomach ulcers and migraines plagued my elementary school days. I lay stone-faced through many sleepless nights, afraid to face the truth for fear it might devour me. I lost all sense of security and self-worth. I felt like crying all the time but the tears wouldn't come.

Confusion and fear stalked my mind like a dragon for much of my life—sharp talons of emotional pain tattooing my heart and mind, marking me. While I tried to deny the pain, its venom manipulatively poisoned every choice I made.

When emotional pain is left untreated
it mutates, ravages the soul.

When We Struggle to Connect

The fallout of such pain offered me a couple life lessons. One, men could not be trusted, especially fathers. Two, community was a lie, and it hurts—family and friends who were supposed to love and protect you, were instead controlling and selfish. Combined, these lessons taught me that I was better off on my own. It was safer that way.

When we stifle the need for connection,
we sacrifice a healing intimacy and companionship,
forfeiting the opportunity to unfold that
which cannot be discovered in solitude.

For years, I washed down an agonizing heart–pain. I stuffed my hurts, swallowing hard my feelings to avoid facing them. But once ignored, these hurts morphed into a toxic anger. A cynical hypersensitivity took root in my soul, emotionally isolating me from anyone that I suspected might bring pain.

To complement my aloneness, I mastered the art of pretense. I became a workaholic, drowning myself in details, pushing beyond all limits—a classic overachiever. Rewarded with many accolades and enviable promotions, I ignored the pain. It was easier that way.

My career took off. And that was good. I was valuable, needed. That alone was worth it.

But I was lonely. So very lonely. Even in the company of others, I still felt isolated. I spent my first forty years in failed relationships; I lost count of the heartbreaks. Healthy, intimate connections required trust, and my father had stolen that years ago.

I won't risk it. Not again. I can't stand the thought of being hurt or not being good enough, of failing again. Besides I have more time this way—more freedom to pursue the things I want, things friends would only pull me away from.

Friends and relationships with others were like a hot stove that could scorch a fierce burn with one mishap. So I avoided them. I built hard, high walls to keep people from knowing the real me. But the walls somehow knew they were a mere fabrication. An illusion of control. In anger, those walls turned on me; if I was going to keep people out, they would keep me in.

We've not changed much since Eve, have we? These lies I believed—they carried me right out of the garden to a place of painful thorns and thistles. I could have had love, intimacy, divine connection, but instead I chose to hide.

Thankfully, Jesus came looking for me.

Oh, I'd known about Jesus for a long time—I have a praying mother who'd made sure of that. For years, I made the traditional church trips on Easter and Christmas to appease Mom. But there was no relationship with Jesus, no intimate link, and certainly no evidence of real joy or true freedom in my life.

It was a father-block. Do you know how hard it is to comprehend a loving God as father when you've gone all your life without one?

But those token trips were a starting point, seedlings for a garden of hope that would one day burst with beautiful life. Those trips introduced me to a Son instead of a father figure. A loving and merciful Jesus was a little easier for me to accept, to open up to.

Years of silent screams pressed upward, begging for release in the dawn of this new safe place with Jesus. *Could this be what I've been missing? What my heart craves? Is there really someone who wants me and loves me just the way I am? Someone who won't use my past against me or twist my personality into a mere reflection of themselves?*

What do we do when we finally meet "the one"? We go all-in. I wanted to *know* Jesus, what he thought and said, how he spent his time, and who he hung out with. So I turned to his "journal," immersing myself in the Bible to find out as much as I could as quickly as I could.

It was here, in the shadow of Jesus and his friends, that I first sampled the healing power that sits within authentic community. I discovered that many of Jesus' women friends were battle-scarred, soul-wounded. I no longer felt invisible. *There are women like me. Women who understand what I've been through.* All my life I had longed to be understood, known, and now Jesus introduced me to women who got it. Who knew the pain. As I dug deeper into their lives, the hope of new beginnings stirred. In time, my biggest fear somehow became my deepest craving: real relationship. But would I, could I, be real? Could I dive that deep? Would I drop my painted masks and reach out for friendship?

It's hard to start over. Hard to be deeply seen and known, to trust others with our hearts when we've been hurt. Will they run? Misunderstand? Ridicule even? Or maybe, just maybe, they can help restore what was once lost?

> *Life as a poser we understand.*
> *But the day the desire to become what*
> *we had only pretended to be*

wages war against our pretender-selves—
That is the day real life begins.

When There Is No Substitute for Face Time

"It's time—hurry up! Be quiet. Stay out of sight, or else." Carol's mother forced her and her siblings beneath two single beds. It was stifling hot, humid, and hard to breathe—an awful place to be stuck on a sunny afternoon.

Tucked in the attic, the children didn't dare allow any sound to escape. That upper room, with sloped ceiling-walls, sat on the creaky second floor of the two-bedroom home at the corner of Magnolia and Cherry Streets. Passers-by couldn't know that six children sat captive there beneath two tiny beds. Even though two windows in the room offered light, the curtains remained drawn and the door shut when their mother had company. The children, two boys and four girls from four to seventeen years old, were banished to the attic-room most weekends, and isolated for days, sometimes months.

In order to keep her boyfriends around, the overwhelmed single mother denied having the children. Trying to keep them secret, she forced the children to remain hidden any time she had a date in the house. With an abusive, alcoholic father who had long ago abandoned them, the children were accustomed to fending for themselves.

Taught early how to lie, and about the importance of family secrets, Carol was silenced for years. But worse was the *invisible silence*—the one that built an unrelenting pressure, nurtured a bitter rage.

Abandoned and desperate for acceptance, Carol fell prey to waiting predators. Scars from rapes, an abortion, and multiple affairs (just like her mother) marked her, claiming her heart.

"Longing to be loved, I would do *anything* to please people. I compromised myself, having sex simply to gain favor and acceptance. In the name of love, I settled for even more abuse while mentally escaping through drugs and alcohol. I didn't want to feel anything—feeling worthless was bad enough," Carol said.

The more you nurture a negative memory,
the stronger it becomes—testing you, mocking you,
freezing you to a pain you may repeat,
in spite of vowing otherwise.

After years of an addictive cycle, Carol broke. "God, help me," she begged.

At twenty-three years old, those simple words changed her life. Through a caring elderly stranger, Carol met and fell in love with Jesus. When she learned how much God loved her, how much he valued her, the soul-corroding shame lost its power.

With a new focus, Carol headed off to a private Christian college in Tennessee. "I was hungry for a new and better way to live," she said. "For the first time, I was surrounded with strong, wise mentors and passionate friends—all seeking to know God and his Word."

No longer invisible, no longer silent, Carol continues her quest, as she recently completed a master's degree in ministry leadership and now serves in a coaching and teaching ministry.

How does one heal such unimaginable hurts? How very painful to be abused by those who should have instead loved and nurtured. A hurt like this corrupts our minds, tempting us to reject ourselves, lose ourselves.

Outside of Jesus, everything that enters our lives re-encounters our original hurts, the trauma acting as a filter of ongoing rejection and pain. And then there's this constant drive to understand, to somehow compensate.

When we're desperate for acceptance,
needy for a love we never experienced,
we discount the real person inside,
damaging our heart and wounding our souls.
We waste our voices.

At times, my own neediness has caused me to manipulate circumstances. I am the ultimate Serenity Prayer failure. Not a fan of accepting things I cannot change.

I want and need people to love me—or at the very least, like me. In pursuit of that acceptance, I have exhausted myself many times. (What I really need is to stop being so needy, to stop doubting my worth.)

While this original need for love and connection is valid—God created us that way—we have to be careful not to substitute, not to waste our time on things to try to fill our need for love.

Things like taking on extra tasks when we know we don't have the time, because, well, she asked, and what would it look like if I told her no. Or that perfect dress we found on clearance that simply had to have matching shoes, and the electric bill wasn't technically late until next week anyway.

And oh, we couldn't possibly throw away that leftover cake after they spent so much time making it, right? Or ignore those Facebook notifications of hurting women that ding through on our phones even though we promised the kids a family night tonight. And what about that miniature bottle we found hidden in the top of the pantry; the one we thought we'd thrown away after the last binge.

When life's not working, when we feel we have nowhere or no one to turn to, we tend to look for an experience that will somehow fix things. I wonder, do you have an activity that you use to substitute for a lack of acceptance, friendship, or love?

Why We Need Intimate Communion, Even When We Hurt

I'm a lot like Eve. So much that it frightens me. I've walked my own garden, made my choices that disconnected me from God. I, too, have believed that it's better to hide, to lie, than to risk the necessary work of genuine intimacy.

I fear being found out. Fear being known. Fear being exposed for who I really am. Naked and afraid, I hide under my perfected and polished fig leaf.

For years, I sat quietly hiding my deepest emotions from others, and worse, from myself. The lack of relationship paralyzed me, riddling me with insecurity and hopelessness.

Under the guise of busyness, my one-on-one interaction grew more limited each day. I did everything online—bill paying, banking, even shopping for a new husband. I filled my car with gas and paid with a single swipe. Picked up freshly pressed laundry from one drive-through right before I grabbed dinner from another—my lack of chatter rewarded with quicker service.

I fear these weeds of disconnection that grow in our relational gardens. Thanks to the ability to manage friendships from our phones and tablets, we have hundreds, even thousands, of folks we consider friends that stretch worldwide.

But this vortex of online community is a perfect set up for soul–wounded women, tempting us with a false sense of connection—a disjointed perception of value and worth. Do you ever feel important simply because you're surrounded by "friends" and an e-mail box that's packed? (Or maybe worse, unimportant because you don't?)

We tell ourselves we're in intimate relationships, but these online friendships with their typed-out, well-crafted responses have no risk. The interaction is too safe. Real relationship requires you to be, well, real.

Now, I'm a big fan of social media. Love it. I have a ton of online friends, and I love them. God has connected me with absolutely amazing women online—beautiful women I may never have met otherwise. But for us, the deeper relationship comes when my friends and I intentionally pull offline, when we set a date for a hands-on, real-time connection.

There is nothing that replaces the open-hearted power
of a live, intimate conversation
with a trusted friend.

How many friends do you have who *really* know you? I mean, the sort of relationship that a girlfriend could walk unannounced into your home at any point and you wouldn't be tempted to take cover.

Hiding won't protect our hearts forever.
No matter how high our walls,
someone will eventually find us.

That link we have with Jesus—that also links us to each other. God designed us for intimate community with each other. He wants us to do life together, sharing both our successes and our struggles.

The early church embraced and modeled this concept; they called it *koinonia*. The classical Greek word meant "full sharing." This was their norm—their way of survival, really. Doing everything together. Crying. Laughing. Struggling. Celebrating.[7]

I get it—opening up like this can be a risk. A big one.

There are those times we become our masks, convince ourselves we actually are what we've pretended to be. To answer this call to "full sharing" of our selves, the masks must come off. And depending on how attached we are to them, that could cause some pain.

But without this willingness to be open, we sacrifice trusted communication. Intimate connections that can bring healing. Without the risk, we miss the reward of a relationship that allows us to truly be ourselves. Real and raw, no masks required.

My friend Lisa Buffaloe is a great example of this *koinonia*. Lisa and I encourage each other's dreams, nurture hurts, and hold one another accountable. She's the sort of friend who texts regularly just to make sure I'm good. Sometimes she'll drop a card in the mail, offer a virtual hug through e-mail, or might even leave a prayer on my phone. We have a solid, comfortable, trusting, and open relationship.

But we didn't start out that way. After connecting and discussing some common interests and life events, we pinged back and forth, serving small portions of information at a time—testing one another.

Are you safe?

Yes, I'm safe—are you safe?

Over time, we grew as friends. We nurtured a mutual desire to go deep, to speak into each other's lives. This freedom allowed us to link our hearts, our stories, to be *known*. That's the "full sharing" God intends.

Dr. Larry Crabb, famous for his lifelong work in psychotherapy, believes the deep wounds of our souls can be healed within intimate community. That something powerful happens when believers authentically connect.

> Something is poured out of one and into the other that has the power to heal the soul of its deepest wounds and restore it to health. . . . Christians have been given resources that if released could powerfully heal broken hearts, overcome the damage done by abusive backgrounds, encourage the depressed to courageously move forward, stimulate the lonely to reach out . . . and introduce hope in the lives of countless people who feel rejected, alone, and useless.[8]

When believers connect, "something is poured out of one and into the other that has the power to heal." Yes! Through honest vulnerability with *trusted* friends (or counselors) we uncover a deep emotional connection that stirs healing.

I hope your heart is pressing you to connect, even if you've been hurt. Especially if you've been hurt. My mama-heart wants to hold you close, even now, and promise you that this works if you risk it.

But I also want to add a caution. For, as much as I want you to experience the healing power of community, I know there are some who can latch to your wound of loneliness in a negative way, having the potential to hurt you deeper still.

The Art of Exploiting Wounds

Elizabeth, a preacher's daughter, data analyst, and single mom now actively involved in ministry, understands the lure of substitutes, having fallen to the promise of community found within a gang during her college years.

Unsuspecting, and with unmet needs, Elizabeth was enticed into a sense of belonging. With their own rules and laws, the gang adhered to a "code of ethics" that played into her need for acceptance.

> *"Who keeps you safe? Takes care of you? Pays for your college? We want to do that for you," the gang leader said.*
>
> *I had just survived a brutal attack that left me pregnant, and was working five part-time jobs to get through school. The dangling security appealed to me.*
>
> *Raised in church as a pastor's daughter, I felt alone. Isolated. I didn't ever fit in. I had no sense of community in the churches my dad served in. No one wanted to come to a "pastor's house" to play, and it wasn't cool to invite the "pastor's daughter" to a party.*
>
> *I was broken. My sense of love skewed at a very young age because of sexual abuse. The shame and secrecy of that abuse caused me to feel like an outsider in my own home. When the walls caved, I turned to the gang. They offered me my first sense of belonging, seemingly accepting me for who I was while my church experiences merely fed a facade.*
>
> *Finally, I felt safe from any more strangers attacking me on the streets. Our gang had guns, and they knew how to use them.*
>
> *My financial worries disintegrated—I'd never known such financial security in my life. My tuition, room, and board were taken care of. I had new clothes whenever I wanted and a car whenever I needed. But these things came at a cost. At that point, I didn't realize how high the cost. My brokenness numbed me to the intimacy involved in the act of sex. This helped me to survive the initiation in the beginning, and later, being pimped out.*
>
> *It wasn't until many years later (when I became part of a healthy church family) that I recognized how insane the sense of*

community in that gang was. Gangs are merely an entrepreneurial venture. They spot a need for a sense of security and latch on. They met my financial needs. They exploited my brokenness and yet made me feel loved in the process—even if it was a false sense of love.

It took the experience of authentic belonging (relationship) within the body of Christ for me to recognize and heal from the dysfunction of what gangs present as community—a community much easier to get into than escape out of.

We aren't the only ones afraid of being hurt. Most everyone is fearful of being hurt in some way, and unfortunately some people hurt others to keep from being hurt themselves. While you may have never been exploited by a gang like Elizabeth, the dysfunction of false community plays out pretty much the same. An unhealthy emptiness or a "used-up" feeling caused by the inner strife and pain of another person is a strong indication that person isn't a good candidate for healthy community.

Substitutes are a waste of our time, and hearts.

How to Choose Right Community

To experience this joy that comes from healing community, we must choose wisely. It's a healthy connection we want, one of prayer, faith, hope, and spiritually discerned grace. Relationships where we can stand shoulder-to-shoulder and heart-to-heart while we learn to overcome life's hurts. Anything outside of this is a diseased imitation and we should avoid it.

Where are they—these healthy relationships? How do we find them?

- **Pray.** Please don't start the journey without this simple yet crucial step: pray for God's leading. I shudder when I consider the poor relationships I could have avoided if only I had prayed first. When we seek new relationships without asking God for direction, it's like telling him we don't need his guidance. Trust me—we do.

- **Prepare our hearts.** Are we ready to deal with some heart-issues, even if it means exposing our wounds to allow for their healing? We can't do this out of sheer willpower. We have to mentally and spiritually position ourselves for God to do this transforming work in us. Only he can strengthen our hearts for what's to come.

- **Be on the lookout.** We want to be in relationship with someone who knows how to pray, knows God's Word, and knows how to accept guidance from him. Watch for women who have demonstrated spiritual maturity. Then, watch for an opportunity to connect with them. Sometimes it's as simple as saying, "Hey, I'm struggling in this area, and I wondered if we might talk for a few minutes."

- **Pay attention to the stirrings of our hearts.** If someone new approaches with an interest in connecting, that might be God. *Ask him.* Or, if there is a particular woman we respect, maybe, just maybe, we could invite her to coffee and open up a little. Won't you take a second, even now to jot down someone you could possibly confide in?

- **Set our boundaries in advance.** While we ourselves need to stay in the Word for balance, we also need to hold our friends/mentors accountable to Scripture. Do their insights and counsel line up with what the Bible says? (Let's not be so desperate for friends that we forget this accountability.)

- **Consider our expectations.** The relationship should have a spiritual focus and should be intentional. Not a gripe session, but rather a chance to establish a bond with a trusted friend who can help us unearth any obstacles that block us from God's plans.

- **Check our mind-sets/attitudes.** Are we receptive, willing to receive counsel? If there's a twinge inside of us as we read the benefits of authentic community, a spark that says "I want that," that's a good sign.

- **Do not hide.** We have to make ourselves available. When God opens the door, take the risk of relationship. Step out, no matter how uncomfortable it feels. Drop the masks and get real. And then, watch what God can do.

I realize this may be a little uncomfortable for those of us who have spent our lives running from these very things, but this new direction, these intentional mind-sets, they are what will lead us into the arms of healthy, healing community.

God's Healing Words

Dear Silent One,

I see you, tucked in the corner, battling for obscurity. Defending yourself from life's pain. Afraid to trust. Afraid to feel. But I also recognize that craving in the deep recesses of your heart, the place you won't let others see.

My heart is pierced with your longing to be heard, valued, understood, and appreciated. Actually, I fashioned you that way. It warms my heart to see that desire stirring within you.

I must tell you, though, deficient of the acceptance and love and worth that I have designed for you, your soul will always feel deprived. Like a little girl stuck in an empty pool, you will always be waiting, wondering, wishing someone would come along and give you the water you need to have fun. To be full. To feel alive.

It's time to stop hiding. To venture forth. In spite of what's happened to you, there are safe, godly people who long to help. Who can help. People waiting to pour into you the very resources I have implanted within them. You cannot move into the abundant joy-filled life I have designed for you without these relationships. Within healthy community, you will grow strong and heal. You will learn to use your voice; you will become a Silence-Breaker.

If you cannot bring yourself to trust them, you must trust me. Trust that I have good things in store for you. Hope-filled, purpose-laced days are ahead. Complete restoration, redemption, and a future of success await; it's time to move beyond this pain.

Let's dive deeper. I promise the adventure is worth the risk. Allow me to lead you to others who will love you through this pain. Yes, I am doing something new, but in the midst I will love you and comfort you. I promise. And in the end, I will make you whole.[9]

Love,

Your Creator and Comforter

THE VOICE STUDIO:

Responding to God's Call to Develop Our Voices

Discovering the Healing Connection within Healthy Community

1. Where is your safe place? Where (or to whom) do you turn when you are hurting?
2. Describe a time when you felt the sting of betrayal within the walls of community. How does this impact your relationships now?
3. Do you ever feel like you are the only one with a particular problem? That others would not accept you if they knew what was really going on? How does that impact your ability to engage other women?
4. In what ways do you hide from community? Is connecting with other women easy or difficult for you? Why?

5. Do you find it difficult to trust? If so, why? Are you willing to move beyond any distrust? What intentional steps could you take to help you trust again?
6. Is there someone to whom you feel drawn? Have you connected with her? Why or why not?
7. Is it easier for you to do things for others or to have things done for you? Do you receive as well as you serve?
8. Are you willing to tell the truth in a safe environment? Do you do this now? Why or why not?
9. What do you tend to substitute for community?
10. Has anyone emotionally invested in you before in a healthy manner? What impact did that have on you? Are you willing to receive counsel from someone else now? Identify one person who might be able to encourage you during this season.

3

Quit the Quiet

When Admitting the Pain Unpacks a New Heart-Attitude

The day came when the risk to remain tight in a bud was more painful than the risk it took to blossom.

~**Anais Nin**

"Are you okay, Jo Ann?" My co-worker Karen asked. The warmth of her tone and sincerity of concern loosened the icy fortress around my heart—but only slightly.

"I'm fine, thanks." My voice cracked a little. *Had she noticed?*

"Again, I'm sorry I can't make today's meeting."

"That's all right, we'll manage. But I'm more concerned about you. Are you sure everything is okay?"

"Of course I am. I'm simply not feeling well . . ."

"All right. If I'm crossing any lines just say so but I get this feeling things are really not *okay* with you. Can we talk?"

An unwelcome lump squeezed my heart. *Can we talk? Oh how I long to talk to you. I can't imagine what it would feel like to jerk this mask off and tell you the truth. But I don't dare take that chance.*

I danced my usual steps, somehow managed to satisfy Karen, and politely ended the conversation.

The backlash of this particular incident with my (then) husband was intense. A week had passed since our argument, and no amount of make-up covered the greenish-purple mass above my eyelid, or the handprint still on my arm.

Yet no matter how many times I successfully sidestepped Karen (and others), the harsher reality was that I couldn't afford to lose my job. While eight days of pretty-good excuses had cloaked my secret and allowed me to hide out at home, it didn't eliminate the waiting workload. There were some things only I could do—I was forced to find a way to pick up some files from work.

I doused my face with foundation and powder to hide the stress. Heavy eye shadow peeked out above the frames of my oversize sunglasses. In spite of the warm weather, I donned a long-sleeve blouse. Then later that evening when I was certain everyone had left the office, I drove in to work.

With expansion plans underway, the office was located at the end of a long and narrow gravel drive that wound through a construction site. About three-quarters of the way up, the drive curved sharply left before resting in our parking area.

It was on this curve that I saw Karen leaving work. *Oh no!* I thought. My heart raced with panic. *There is no escape.* Karen pulled her car within inches of mine and rolled down the window.

"There you are. I've been worried about you." There it was again—that sincere concern and soul-penetrating smile.

"Oh, I've been swamped. On top of being sick, my daughter Tabitha is extremely busy with school and activities, plus I've been trying to do some of this work from home without having everything I need—it's been a little crazy." My voice wavered, my words tumbling out much faster than I intended.

"I know I've asked before," Karen said, "but are you *really* okay, Jo Ann?"

Excruciating silence hung in the air for a full minute.

My stomach squashed into a little ball. The familiar yet terrifying primal need to share the truth welled up once again within me.

Can I trust you, Karen? I've been hurt so many times by my husband and by others who only feigned friendship. Why would you care about me?

Like a fragile flower rushed to open up by an unusually warm spring, my resistance gave way. Without a word, I broke the silence by lifting my sunglasses. In spite of the cosmetic rendering, Karen could easily see the trauma to my face. The broken blood vessels and inflammation around my eye told a story my words would not.

I waited for the judgment. The shock. The disbelief and condemnation.

"I'm so sorry, Jo Ann." Karen's eyes welled with tears. "Do you want to talk about it?"

"Maybe later." I quickly slid my glasses back onto my face, uneasy from the revelation and wanting so badly to escape her gaze, her obvious concern. This was enough connecting for now.

"Just know that I'm here—and I care deeply." Karen waited, window rolled down, while I pulled off.

Later, I felt an unexpected relief from sharing my secret; somehow the grip of anxiety around my heart lessened. But it wasn't without consequence. I could no longer pretend everything was fine. Karen had fractured my façade.

What now? What did Karen really think of me? Who would she tell?

Those Times We Can No Longer Remain Silent

There are raw, painful places inside every one of us that stem from some degree of rejection, insecurity, or shame. Places we'd like to keep hidden. But I challenge you to find at least one safe person—whether a counselor, friend, relative, mentor, or pastor—committed to seeing you healed. (And refuse to believe the lie that there is no one. God already has someone in mind.)

Though ones selfish and unstable
have siphoned your childlike trust,
I dare you to honor the ache that yet hopes
for nontoxic and loving relationships.

For years I denied these hidden places, these hurts. That's what we're supposed to do, right? Stuff those sort of things, pretend we're okay with them?

But Karen's safety sparked a desire in me to open up. Little by little, my story leaked out. My deep-rooted fear of never measuring up. Of being rejected. The shame of the years I lived with abuse.

When my story finally unfolded in this safe place with Karen, it was as if I was hearing it new, facing these words of truth for the first time. Karen never tried to push me out of the marriage, but she did let me know it wasn't a safe environment and that there was help available when I was ready. Her divinely inspired never-forget-I-care attitude nurtured a newfound courage within me. I risked vulnerability, and in turn experienced genuine friendship for probably the first time.

Twelve years later, my shoulders regularly sink into the leather grain of my now-best-friend's couch. My friendship with Karen is ever-growing and continually transforming. We've walked together hand-in-hand, heart-to-heart through my divorce from that abusive marriage, my remarriage to a godly man, and through the birth of a new ministry where I willingly pour myself, raw and real, into the lives of others.

Fear had convinced me that silence was the safest way out of that abusive situation. That was a lie. Unfortunately, I'm not the first to believe that lie. I imagine you, too, have been intimidated or shamed into silence at some point. Maybe not an abusive silence, but silence still. I also imagine that must really hurt God's heart—when we believe what we have to say isn't important or valued.

A forced silence is a dangerous imposter,
painting a canvas of safety
while plotting our demise.

I wonder what would happen if we all just took off our masks and spoke our truths. Can you imagine how liberating it would feel if life on the outside could actually line up with the person on the inside?

That's God's plan for us. He longs for us to be who we really are. To find and use our real voices. Our voice matters—it's a valuable gift from God, and is designed to be used.

The Courage to Open the Story-Door

There are many women in the Bible to whom I relate, but for this season of my life I feel a deep kindred spirit with the woman who suffered a blood issue.[10] For over seven years, I have battled an often debilitating chronic illness that could not be diagnosed. My husband and our insurance company have wasted thousands of dollars trying to identify and solve the problem.

Test after inconclusive test returned, until about two years ago when the Mayo Clinic and a local hematologist determined I had a genetic *gift*—a rare blood disorder that manifests neurologically. Why we spent so much money to obtain that diagnosis I can't justify, now that we've discovered the only treatment is an invasive port that administers a medicine that merely treats the symptoms but doesn't cure the problem. The same medicine that has historically been responsible for countless episodes of kidney failure and blood clots. Not a fan of that idea.

Much like the woman with the issue of blood, we spent a lot of money on physicians with no real resolution. My primary physician debates the diagnosis, so there remains some doubt. But if there is humor in any of this, it's the reaction I get when some people discover I may have a blood disease. They don't really know how to form the question that lingers on their tongues: "Is it contagious?" Some even step back—as if sixteen inches of separation provides some sort of protection.

My anxious friends miss an important part, though: this particular malady is genetic, not contagious. It is simply a dysfunction in the way the body produces the chemicals that help the production of hemoglobin (that oxygen-carrying component of red blood cells). The fallout, for me, is agonizing, gnawing, excruciating neuropathy along with occasional cognitive issues that can't be treated successfully by any sort of medication. But it's a malfunction, not some communicable disease.

Because of this "genetic gift," I experience these moments (thankfully rarely) where I feel a little shunned. But this uneducated cold-shouldering is nothing like the scorning of my biblical friend. The one who couldn't even show her face in public without fear of being stoned.

Talk about making people nervous. Her neighbors wanted nothing to do with her for fear of contamination. This poor woman didn't just have a physical problem; she had a social problem and a religious problem to contend with as well.[11] But Jesus wasn't afraid to interact with her. To love her, value her. This woman had heard that Jesus could heal her and was determined to break through. She risked reproach, ridicule, public humiliation, and her very life.

Jesus did heal her. But not just her physical illness. Because Jesus values a woman's voice, I believe he wanted her to understand that if she would speak from her heart, she would experience an encounter much more meaningful than any physical healing. So he called her out, forcing her to publically acknowledge her situation.

Now there's a crash course in sharing our stories with others.

"Who touched me?" Jesus asked. He knew who had touched him—that wasn't the issue. This was a spiritual initiation for a woman whose healing story had the power to change community.

After spending twelve years with an unknown illness, after bearing unfathomable rejection and shame, this brave woman risked death once again as she knelt at the feet of Jesus to share her story. A story that undeniably strengthened the faith of the new believers in the crowd.

When We Stumble into Freedom's Brightness

As Karen and I grew in relationship, one of the greatest gifts she gave me was validation. Her genuine interest in me (hurts, hang-ups, and all) cradled my heart with compassion, nurturing my soul with a connection I had never previously felt.

It's something we all long for, especially when we're hurting inside. Acceptance. Approval. Confirmation that we somehow matter. Ultimately, true validation has to come from God, yes, but healthy recognition sure warms a wounded heart.

Unaware, I had carried my childhood perspective into adult relationships: *Love doesn't reach out—it hurts, rejects, kills. It is a deception, a prison.* As manic as it sounds, I needed someone to tell me it wasn't normal to be treated the way I was being treated. That my hopes for a different life, healthy relationships, weren't crazy.

It took someone like Karen to help me understand that I deserved healthy love and safe relationship. Will you allow me to stir that within you as well? Help you see that you are worthy of the same? This may seem obvious for some, but there are those who feel like I did, those who have been lied to their whole lives about who they are and what they deserve. This truth may be a healing balm, pouring over the core of their souls as they accept that someone else's opinion of them doesn't have to be their reality.

Please don't ever be fooled into thinking you deserve any type of abuse. I know your abuser may say otherwise (oh, how I know), but the Lord despises this cruelty.[12] You are valuable, loveable, and loved—deserving of God's best in your life.

Will you, this moment perhaps, ask God to send you a hands-on advocate—someone willing to come alongside you in this journey who can remind you of this truth?

When Silence Infects Us with Doubt

Laura Hyers is a beautiful young newlywed who recently graduated with a bachelor's in psychology. Laura is one of our columnists for *Write Where It Hurts*, a virtual community that has become a popular online gathering place for Christian women to process the hard stuff that surfaces daily.

Like most of us, Laura tends to close herself off when she's been hurt—the silence choking her heart, the pleasantries and small talk pushing away depth and intimacy with others. It's hard to open your heart to new relationships when the pain of the old ones threaten like a river about to burst the banks.

This intentional choice to share our pain
requires us to forgive those who have hurt us;
the doubts and insecurities a finery for hope.

Laura recently blogged about a forgivingness that can lead to healthier relationships.

Circumstances and perspective can make forgiveness seem impossible. Sometimes we think forgiveness is another word for "deciding all is okay and going back to the way things were before (insert thing being forgiven here) happened."

I know I'm supposed to forgive, but I find myself pleading, Can't I just leave them alone? Can't they just leave me alone?

Yet here's what the Lord revealed to me, through time and pain and healing and (you guessed it) forgiveness: forgiveness does not necessarily mean things return to the way they were.

Forgiveness does not mean the people who have proven themselves untrustworthy are welcomed back with open arms, told the family secrets, given privileged information. The gossip will likely continue to run her mouth, and the abuser may still attempt to raise his hand against you.

Forgiveness does not mean a willingness to put ourselves into dangerous positions. Protect yourself, use good sense, and go to the Lord in prayer about what your relationship with the person you need to forgive will look like—or if there will be a real relationship at all.

> *The Lord is righteous and pursues justice for his children, but his version of justice rarely looks like ours. Throwing away the scorecard of hurts done to you can be the beginning of a beautiful healing process.*

I don't discount this is hard; some wrongs feel simply too overwhelming, the sadness spilling into these waves of hypersensitivity that reverberate far and wide. The suggested offering of forgiveness hovering, senseless, in the air. Seeming such a gross injustice to reduce making peace with our brokenness to one simple statement: I forgive you.

Yet the words hold an unexpected blessing.

Just the other day, Donald Miller tweeted about this, "From an honest understanding of your wounds, and a heart of forgiveness, will come your greatest voice."[13]

Consider that—forgiveness as the pathway to freedom, the passage to uncovering your voice. Granted, that voice might shake at first use, but it is here, in this place of forgiveness, that our voices are first set free.

The part that may well be the hardest? Showing up. If we show up, make the choice to forgive, God will do the work as only he can. But *we* have to be willing to let go. The Greek word for forgive actually means "letting go." That's an active process, one that we make possible by showing up.

Breaking Free

For years I struggled with forgiving both my father and ex-husband. *Grudges are so much easier than grace.* I'm a lot like Laura, because forgiveness can be really, *really*, hard when it's my turn. (Maybe you, too, still have an experience or memory that makes you feel as if you've been drenched in an acid bath?)

Forgiveness as the pathway to freedom, the passage to finding our voices.

Pretending won't get this done—ask me how I know. This is not the sort of forgiveness that we use as an excuse to never properly deal with something. (*Oh, I forgive you—let's just not talk about that anymore.*)

Sometimes it's hard to imagine the beautiful and powerful work God has in store with this forgivingness, but a young man named David understood.

As the first king of Israel, Saul had quickly established himself as an effective military leader for Israel. But the dark side, and I imagine the downfall for Saul, was his unstable emotions and his tendency to compromise. Eventually, Saul's anxiety drove him to search for a musician to ease his troubled heart, and that's where he met our man David.[14]

A young David was appointed to serve Saul, spending many nights strumming a tune to ease Saul's anxious thoughts. The king was refreshed, and David, honored to help. It was a good thing for both of them.[15]

But David was not just a musician, he was also a courageous warrior, and that sort of thing rises up. Soon David was promoted to a high-ranking leadership position.

Courage embraces our vulnerabilities,
shines the light through their haze,
illuminating a path to things we may not
otherwise be able to find.

Here's where it gets uncomfortable. David was one of those "connecty" folks we've talked about—he had a huge base of friends who supported him and celebrated his achievements. So much so, that Saul grew insanely jealous over the amount of attention lavished on David. And Saul decided to kill him. Just like that.

Local favorite David, the poet and mighty warrior who had won the hearts of the Israelites, suddenly found himself hunted down by a deranged king—reduced to the confines of a cave in a hot, Judean desert.[16]

The very same cave that Saul later stepped into in order to relieve himself. *Could a man be any more vulnerable?*

During his moment of rest, Saul had no idea David was tucked beside him in those craggy walls. What prime opportunity for David; he could kill Saul right here, eliminate any fears of the future, and get on with his life. And David's support group was all for it, "This is the day. You can do whatever you want to him."

An emotion-driven vengeance is a poor substitute
for a God-directed justice.
Though revenge tempts us with instant gratification,
it is the sweetness of forgiveness
that ultimately quenches our pain.

> *David said to Saul . . . , "This very day with your very own eyes you have seen that just now in the cave God put you in my hands. My men wanted me to kill you, but I wouldn't do it. . . . I haven't sinned against you, and yet you're hunting me down to kill me. . . . God may avenge me, but it is in his hands, not mine. An old proverb says, 'Evil deeds come from evil people.' So be assured that my hand won't touch you."*[17]

I spared you. David basically tells Saul, "I let it go—left it in God's hands."

While he couldn't control Saul's choices, he could take responsibility for his own. A clean heart was a much greater priority to David than revenge. And I suspect the very moment he relinquished the need for gratification that Saul's abusive ways lost their power over him.

That abundant life God has in store for us?
It can be eclipsed by self-pity.
The bad things we have walked through
do not have to dictate
our tomorrow.

Admit the Pain and Unpack a New Heart-Attitude

It's hard not to harbor bitterness when you've been hurt. That dark, deep-rooted hatred for my father—for years I didn't recognize it. Until one day, in innocence, a young Tabitha asked about the grandfather she'd never seen. I had somehow convinced myself she would require no explanation. She had a paternal grandfather who was great, a positive influencer. Why bother explaining the absence of a not-so-good one?

But now, with one question, I sat with the same bitter nausea of earlier years rising in my throat.

Her grandfather? My churning stomach recoiled at the bite of her words. *The thought that she would call a man who had sexually abused me her grandfather?*

I offered some lame excuse about his premature death that satisfied her, until a few more years brought us face-to-face with the aftershocks of my young life. One day, Tabitha uncovered a feature I'd written that shared the story of the abuse I had suffered at the hands of my father. She had lots of questions for me—questions I wasn't ready for.

I wish I could say I gently sat her down and explained how God's grace covers a multitude of sins, how the same Jesus who died for her also died for my father. And how, in our humanity, in a fallen world, we are all, unfortunately, capable of evil to some degree.

I did not. I spewed vicious, hurtful words about his atrocious behavior which planted seeds of hatred, fear, and confusion in her teenage heart for a man she never knew.

And I'm a Christian. A Christian taught to forgive.

Well-meaning pastors, counselors, and friends had urged me to forgive. But I refused to be "tricked" into excusing wrong behavior. Until forgiveness was something I could offer from the heart, I had no use for it.

"Someday, God." I made a dangerous promise.

Solely out of fear of eternal punishment I repeatedly promised God that I would one day forgive. "Someday" was easier to digest. It was "out there"—an elusive future promise, a temporary protection.

But God calls me (calls us) to forgive now. Today. In this go-round on earth.

Eventually, I surrendered the work to him. On my own, I simply couldn't yield my right to vengeance, my need to understand, or even the anger that so weakly camouflaged my pain. Motivated by my love for God, just as I chose Christ as my Savior, I had to choose, in faith, to forgive my father. That's just God's way.

God honored my choice. Quietly, without me even knowing, he worked in my heart as days passed.

A couple of months later I stood in my kitchen, alone in the house with my husband out of town. The aroma of freshly chopped garlic signaled me to turn on the stove. Momentarily distracted, I watched the black stovetop surface bleed into vibrant color. Flame red. A random thought scorched my mind. *Would my father spend forever in hell—is he possibly there now?* Tears formed, then trickled down. With Christ's heart in me, I no longer wanted revenge. I wouldn't wish the ravages of hell on any man—even the man who had brought so much pain in my own life.

I put the meal on hold, and went to God in prayer.

> *Father, for years I've struggled with this issue of forgiveness—as if forgiveness somehow makes what my father did acceptable. It's not acceptable Lord. And in my human mind, I can't comprehend or allow forgiveness of this man. What he did was wrong, excruciatingly painful on so many levels. But Lord, I guess I've done bad things too. I've turned away from you and I have hurt people. And I don't want that to stand in the way of my own forgiveness. Just as I am your child, so is he. Please grant him your mercy. Help me to grant him mercy, as well.*

A language doesn't exist to describe the feeling; it was beyond my comprehension or natural ability. Corrie ten Boom, a Nazi concentration camp survivor, aptly describes what felt other worldly to me. "Forgiveness is to set a prisoner free, and to realize the prisoner was you."

Forgiveness didn't excuse my father after all, certainly didn't say, "What you've done is okay" or "I will continue to let you hurt me." But I was changed, and a power was released—a power that healed a very painful life hurt. A power that extended grace. God's grace. A Silence-Breaking grace that heals and restores.

A lack of forgiveness robs us of the trust
God wants us to have in him.

God's Healing Words

Dear Silence-Breaker,

No one would notice unless you said anything. But I see. I see how life hasn't worked out as you planned. I see how it's getting harder to pretend, harder to stay quiet—and that's a good thing.

It's time for a change. Please believe me when I tell you that you can trust me. That the truths you find in my Word will help you to change your thinking. And that when you change how you think, line up your thoughts with the way I do things, you will change your life.

Please accept my grace. Walk in the fullness of it. Yes, I am fully aware of these bad things that have happened to you, and I even know the bad things you've done. But I want to wash you clean, relieve you of that terrible guilt and shame.

Let me help you heal from the betrayal of others who have cut you deeply. Release to me your desire for revenge, your need of explanation.

This same grace I offer you, offer to the ones who have hurt you. The grace to forgive, to release. It is more for you than them. I have a work to do, you have work to do, and this bitterness blocks you from this work—blocks you from me.

I will redeem this, use it for my good, I promise. And I can heal you so deeply that no one could ever tell you were hurt. But you must surrender this pain to me.

Set aside any protective masks that block others from reaching you. Please trust the healing advocates I send you. Let your once-silent mouth begin to shout for joy as water springing up from desert land. Share your truth in this safe place, and begin to heal. Trust me with these places. Even though none of this makes sense to you right now, I have a plan. And it's good. I promise.[18]

Love,

Your Deliverer and Healer

THE VOICE STUDIO:

Responding to God's Call to Develop Our Voices

Confronting the Silence

1. Are you tolerating something you shouldn't? What do you need to do about it? How are you (maybe unknowingly) "allowing" this behavior? How can you stop it? How can you set up a support system to overcome it?
2. What secret do you wish you could make known? Do you think sometimes it's easier *not* to say anything?
3. What would your life be like if the person you are on the outside lined up with the emotions and actions of the person on the inside?
4. Being honest about your hurts is very important. Make a list of your hurts. Then, beside each one, list one thing that you think is blocking your healing in that area.
5. We hear this talk of an abundant life; what do you imagine that is? How does a forced silence keep us from living one?

6. Did you pray for God to send you a friend for your journey—a hands-on advocate to remind you of truth? Why or why not?
7. Is there someone you find difficult to forgive? Who, and why haven't you been able to release the pain?
8. Imagine you are the person who has caused you emotional pain. Write a letter to you from that person, saying what you wish they would say. Be willing to step into the third person so that you can address that person's perspective through their words to you.
9. Do you believe it is easier to forget than forgive? To move on rather than face the pain, the need to forgive?
10. Will you, this minute, pray for God to do a work in your heart that allows you to release any unforgiveness? (I've never known anyone to sincerely pray that prayer and not be changed.)

That Still Small Voice

Developing an Intimate Partnership with God

If you want to find your voice, you need to hear the voice of God.
~Mark Batterson

"Could you hold please while the doctor comes on the line?" the nurse said. Uneasy, I leaned my elbows on the kitchen countertop and cradled the cell phone to my ear.

"Sure . . . " I said. *An unexpected personal call from my doctor? This can't be good.*

After recently experiencing bouts of excruciating abdominal pain, I had gallbladder surgery to remove a lodged gallstone. Unfortunately, what should have been a routine procedure turned into quite the misadventure with serious complications, allergic reactions, and "phantom pain." For the past two weeks, the nurses from the gastroenterologist's office had kept a close watch, walking me through follow-up care.

But this phone call? This was a totally unrelated call from my gynecologist.

"Mrs. Fore," the doctor said. "Your cancer screening returned highly elevated—the highest I've ever seen. The prognosis is not good. It looks like you have ovarian cancer. We need to schedule you for immediate surgery."

What a delivery—don't they teach these guys how to relate bad news in a more soothing manner?

A roaring fear rushed in, consuming most of my cognitive abilities. Lightheadedness overtook me and for a few minutes I couldn't think or move. I mumbled a few disjointed words, and then somehow managed to speak.

"Let me talk with my husband and get back with you to schedule a date."

For the next few days I fell silent, twisting through a thick fog of confusion.

I have cancer, God? Where are you in this? Am I going to die? And how, exactly, am I supposed to share my fears with those I love and still guard their fragile hearts?

I'd never felt so out of control.

Three short weeks after that gallbladder-surgery-gone-bad, I headed to the gynecologist's office for pre-op in preparation for yet another surgery—one to examine and remove cancer. It was a Wednesday morning, and oddly, I felt a prompting to go to church that night. Odd, because I hadn't been to a Wednesday night service in a couple of years. Odder still, it wasn't a pressing to go to my own church, but this impression that I needed to visit a friend's church. (Now and then, we face seemingly nonsensical things that we somehow know to do anyway. This was one.)

With Matt (my new husband) leading, we entered the building to the rhythmic sound of a popular worship song, "Trading My Sorrows," written by Darrell Evans. "I'm trading my sickness / I'm trading my pain / I'm laying it down / for the joy of the Lord."[19]

The words, common as they are to anyone who has attended church for more than a couple years, punctured my anxiety. In a move a little out of his character, Matt turned to me and said, "This song is for you."

Sometimes a timeless truth sneaks in, delivers a profound sense of peace and a newfound purpose. In those moments, though we know

God's plans might not play out like we desire, we come to want his plan more than our own.

Something big was about to happen; I sensed it.

When God's Voice Teaches Us to Hope Forward

My husband takes spiritual leadership seriously. (I love that about him.) Although a religion major with years of ministry behind him, Matt is careful never to presume a divine message, but this time he knew it, and wanted me to know it. *God was speaking.*

We settled into a couple of the burgundy-upholstered chairs toward the back of the church. The remaining lyrics of the worship song captured my heart anew, called it to attention. Freshly filled with a sense of God's reality, I remembered that he was watching; he was right here with me, walking this cancer scare, and somehow he already had this thing figured out.

It was one of those holy, faith-strengthening moments that lose something when you try to articulate the encounter to others. But I knew it, and Matt knew it: God was speaking. Personally. To me. It was an impression deep in my spirit that God wanted me to absorb. A God-wired intuition of sorts.

That night, the pastor taught about a woman whose desperate faith brought healing. Guess who? My friend with the blood issue. Seems God had pressed her spirit too, spoken directly to her. "You are now well because of your faith. May God give you peace! You are healed, and you will no longer be in pain."[20]

It was time for some hem-clutching faith. If only I could find the strength to touch the robe. Was I desperate enough—willing to press through, willing to cling to that same remnant of hope?

I silently prayed for my fragile faith to become strong as iron, for Jesus to become my very real strength—my faith itself. The type of healing-faith that releases a circumstance-overcoming peace, a faith-based belief system capable of overpowering both fear and cancer.

God, lift me from this mess as only you can.

Our time at the church ended that day with me joining in on the crowd's enthusiastic rendition of the faith-filled song, "Because He Lives." Ironic for two reasons: one, I can't sing, and two, I'm not a singer of southern gospel. Even though I live in the Tennessee hills, I tend to be a fan of contemporary worship music.

But not this night. From my corner in the back of the room, I tucked my hand into Matt's, and calmly leaned my head onto his chest as I belted with utmost passion, belief, and a slight southern twang, "Because he lives, I can face tomorrow. Because he lives, all fear is gone. Because I know he holds the future. . . . I'll fight life's war with pain."[21]

God's very real presence had quieted my fears. He *was* in control. Not only did he care deeply about me, he was right here with me. We *were* going to get through this together.

Why the Little Voice inside Our Heads Is Not (Always) Crazy

I have a deep hunger to talk with God. I used to dream of hearing his audible words. Surely I wouldn't second-guess myself if I could actually hear his spoken-out-loud voice like Peter, James, and John did.[22] Even my wicked self-doubt wouldn't have the nerve to confront the cloud-piercing voice of God.

That's what I longed for that night at church, a thick-as-syrup conviction that I could hear God. To know he was with me, and that I knew exactly what he was saying.

A week before the surgery to remove the cancer, that's what I got. It wasn't audible, but I knew it was God. I knew he had spoken to me, and that I had heard him.

That morning, I stood at my kitchen window ready to bargain with God. At this point, I was no longer focused on my own fear; I was more concerned about my sixteen-year-old daughter and my new husband—how my potential death would impact their lives.

Life tends to fall into this unforced, sacred rhythm
when you're facing death.
Prayers change.
Priorities realign.
The heart opens wide.

"Lord, if this is it for me on this earth, you're going to have to let me know because I can't do this alone. How do I assure my family everything is going to be okay if I don't believe it myself?"

In my heart I felt these words, "This illness is not about your death, but rather my glory." The Lord *spoke* to me. I could *hear* his voice, yes, through an impression on my heart but I knew it was him. I rushed to my Bible to see if there was a similar scripture, one that would back up what I felt. (Hearing God should do that, you know, line up with his Word.)

There it was, tucked in the eleventh chapter of John, verse 4, "This sickness is not fatal. It will become an occasion to show God's glory."

The following week when those doctors went in, there were no signs of cancer.

Those times when God's plans intersect with our own desires, moments where he feels most real, those are occasions to show him off.

God wants to speak to us—we *can* hear his voice. Admittedly, an audible word from him isn't necessary (would freak me out, actually) but we can *hear* God's leading as we learn to recognize his voice speaking internally to us.

On this journey to find our own voices,
we must first hear his.

At any given moment, mindless chatter could fill my head. The voice of my father, "Others don't need to know about these things you think hurt—they won't care." Or my sixth-grade crush, Wesley, "Red hair is ugly—you're ugly." Or my high school journalism teacher, Chele Dugger, "I love the way you play with words, Jo Ann. You should write stories."

I easily recognize these voices because of our history together, the conversations we had that burned their way into my memory bank.

So it is with God. Our history with him and our beliefs about him determine what we're willing to "hear" from him. If we're wrong in our concepts, prone to believe lies about him, then his voice will be muffled and distorted, difficult to hear.

A. W. Tozer suggests, "What comes into our minds when we think about God is the most important thing about us."[23] I wonder, is your concept of God based on the things other people have done? Criticism, betrayal, or even abuse cannot cancel the fact that God is good and kind and loves us.

As I write these words, I think of the movie *The Help*. In this movie is a maid, Aibileen, who offers loving affirmations ("You is smart. You is kind. You is important.") to her young charge, Mae Mobley. Aibileen desperately wanted to counter the false voices she knew this little girl was hearing—the condemning and blaming accusations that controlled and intimidated the toddler.

How do you hear God's voice? Does it sound affirming, like Aibileen to Mae, or condemning like Mae's unaffectionate mother? Does it sound like the voice of a kind and beloved Parent or the voice of perpetual disappointment and judgment?

What others have damaged,
God can heal.

Hearing God in Spite of the Pain

"I'll be gone fifteen minutes. When I get back, we'll do something you want to do." Trent Lenderink, an experienced free diver, slipped into the irresistible Blue Lagoon without an oxygen tank.

Soaked in the mystical Jamaican waters, he stopped halfway between the dock and the diving hole to lift his hand and wave goodbye to his wife, Tammy.

Tammy sat on the edge of the water, finishing off her lunch. As the fresh-water springs massaged the warm waters of the Caribbean Sea, she savored the last remaining moments of their vacation. The next day, September 11 (the very day terrorists attacked the United States), they were scheduled to embark on a mission trip together.

In the rocky cove, Tammy watched her husband's head bob for fresh air every few minutes until she got sidetracked with some other snorkelers. Thirty minutes later, she realized she hadn't seen Trent—he'd said he would be back in fifteen minutes.

Where is he! Tammy's eyes strained across the translucent waters, searching for the slightest sign.

A boat came in, circling the lagoon and Tammy waved them down. "Can you help me look for my husband?"

They found nothing. Next, a dive team came, scouring the rest of the day until the search was suspended by darkness. When the team resumed the next morning, Tammy's fears were confirmed as they uncovered Trent's lifeless body.

Freshly widowed Tammy—known as popular Christian recording artist, author, and speaker Tammy Trent—panicked. A shocking numbness raced throughout her body, permeated her mind. She tried to breathe, but couldn't draw a full breath.

My life is forever changed.

In the weeks that followed, Tammy found herself fearfully alone, facing a choice. *Is it okay to hurt? I need to take some time out, get my head straight, but how do I do that with my commitments? What would I say to anyone right now, anyway; what would I offer? I can't even stop crying.*

Unaware at this point if she would ever sing or step onto a platform again, Tammy made time to grieve her loss and to hear from God. She made awkward but steady progress in learning to establish boundaries, learning to say no.

A few years later, Tammy shared with me what those initial days without her husband were like as she carved this path to her new normal.

"I'd struggled before with whether or not I really had a voice—really had something to say—but this was very different. I had no idea how God would rebuild my life, but I needed to rediscover God, and who I was.

"As I shut my door to travel," Tammy continued, "I trusted God would reveal himself to me. I needed that time. I needed to clear a bunch of voices pulling at me. I needed to let the voice of God be the strongest one in my heart and head. During that time, it took every ounce of faith I had to lift my eyes toward heaven and allow God to pick me up out of this dark pit."

Because Tammy held healthy beliefs about God, when she was faced with trauma, her default was to trust him—even if it felt senseless. It was far from easy, but her faith guided her to trust God, encouraged her that his promises were still somehow good and trustworthy.

"It's been in me since the days of my youth group. When I was younger, I practiced the love, grace, and mercy of God. I practiced worshiping God, learning about God, trusting God. I believed it in the good times; would I believe it in the bad? Somehow, it was an automatic response for me. My default. To believe he only had good things for me. I clung to that."

If we can come to a right belief about God,
we can face the really hard stuff—
we can trust that somehow, even in this,
he is still working.

When God Speaks His Purposes for Us

Jesus loves me, this I . . . don't. really. know.

God wants to speak to us. (That should encourage you, not scare you.)

But it's hard to hear God if we don't have an intimate relationship with him. This hearing God, trusting and believing him, it's really about love. Not how much *we* love God, but rather how very much *he* loves us.

When we've been hurt, we're vulnerable to a love-doubt that tends to override God's plans. Oh, we can tell others all about his powerful and unending love, but sometimes we don't grasp it for ourselves.

Consider how much God loves us—so much he calls us *his* children. If you're a mother, or had good parents, you understand the depth of that statement. That's real love—not our love for him, but his love for us. My daughter, no matter how old she gets, will always be my baby. The same with us and God; we are still *his* babies.

Look what he did for us, his children. He created earth, a wonderful thing, and then turned it over to us. Even though our representative, Adam, turned around and gave God's gift to Satan, God thought enough of us to buy it back—and he paid the highest price imaginable, the life of his own son. That's love-unfathomable.

God sent Jesus to this earth so that we could live free. He loves us that much. And he has an ultimate, unchanging purpose for us—a universal purpose as well as an individual purpose. But intimidation and shame are powerful de-motivators, these cousins that try to convince us to live some sort of passive life, rather than actively pursue the vibrant one God has for us.

So much threatens to steal our voices, our purpose: stressors, anxious thoughts, fears, failures. Instead of fighting back, we blame our circumstances. *What good would speaking up do anyway?*

The tears fall. The words fail. *How do you speak from the heart when the heart is broken?*

This, this brokenness that needs truth is why God calls us to intimacy with him. In the nearness of him, we hear him, know what he is saying. Within these boundaries, we not only hear what needs to be heard, but learn to say what needs to be said.

The very meaning of the word *intimate* means to tell, to speak out.[24]

Speak out? Satan's counting on that being too hard for those of us who have been hurt. But when we live with God, converse with him daily, we recognize the responsibility of using our voices. In small ways. In big ways. In small ways that become big. That part is God's responsibility. Our role is the discipline of first hearing God, and then telling his story. Speaking out.

Even now, writing those words challenges me. Because I'm passionate about women overcoming life's hurts, I write stories to give people hope. I love serving women worldwide through my words. But lately, God has nudged me to connect on a different level.

Speaking.

Yes, speaking. Like using my out-loud voice, face-to-face in front of folks.

God apparently forgot I'm a shy writer who labeled that one area off limits to him. Forgot about my early-age humiliation that evoked this silent vow: I will never look like an idiot again.

The thought of a microphone and all eyes on me pushed my panic button.

But God had other plans. "If I tell you to go and speak to someone, then go!" he said. "Don't be afraid."[25]

I wouldn't tell God "no" . . . would I?

After a long and hard-fought emotional battle, I surrendered. God and I agreed about the need to effectively reach more women with his promise of hope. If this is the method, knees shaking, I'm in.

> *There comes a time to stop fearing God's plan*
> *—a flashpoint where we stop thinking about ourselves*
> *and we start thinking about*
> *what we can do for others.*

Hearing the Voice of Truth

In his faithfulness, God led me to the amazing women of Proverbs 31 Ministries, shepherded by Lysa TerKeurst. *She Speaks* is a stellar conference hosted by Proverbs 31 that equips writers, speakers, and ministry leaders to share their heart–message. Just the training I needed to even consider following through with this new commitment.

Before I had time to consider the consequences, I registered. My temporary lapse of sanity also drove me to sign up for the conference's speaker evaluation opportunity. I was required to do two talks in front of a small group of women, talks that would be critiqued by both the peers in my group and a speaker evaluator.

I wanted to shine (recovering perfectionist that I am). I buried myself in preparations, determining to execute the talks flawlessly so that no one would know how scared I really was.

There it was again—that fear of being exposed. Insecurities and an ever-present feeling of inadequacy does that to a girl.

Are you so unaware of God's deep-seated love for you
that the opinion of others
shakes God's purpose in your life?

Remember my fear of failing in front of you? It's because I want you to like me. I like it when you think well of me. But I get into trouble when I choose your liking me over being the me God created me to be. At some point in this journey to learn to speak well, I became more engrossed with the eloquence of my words than the heart of my message. I had forgotten this conference was an opportunity to learn, not a place I had to perform.

"If I speak with a silver tongue, convince a crowd but don't have love, I leave a bitter taste with every word I say." For the next few weeks, the lyrics of For King & Country's "Proof of Your Love" seemed to play every time I stepped in my car.

I thank God for his Spirit within us that leads us back to truth.

You don't know how much I (God) love you.
If you have not fully accepted my love
into your own heart,
how can you pour it into the lives of those
you long to encourage?
How can you carry my presence to others?

God decided to use my husband to speak to me again. (After going many years without it, I love the power, the covering, that comes from a praying husband.) One day, during this same period of time, Matt made his way into my office. "I've got something for you from God."

Now, Matt and I had no previous conversations about the love-work God was doing in my heart.

"God wants you to really understand how very much he loves you," Matt said.

Later that month, I attended two conferences that reinforced the same message from God: *I want you to live in awareness of my great love for you.*

Through a gentle pressing in my spirit, through God's Word, through circumstances, through a song, a conference, and even through my husband, God's voice was consistent. Even though my heart was to lead women into God's presence through my speaking, my fearful insecurities were leading them into me.

The women to whom I spoke would feel what I felt—my performance-driven angst, my perfectionist concerns. But the greatest gift I could give them was not inspiring words; it was God. His love flowing through me. A deep love I hosted because I myself encountered, believed, and lived out of it.

How Do *We Hear God Speak?*

It's daring, isn't it? This idea that we can hear God speak. Just yesterday I was browsing the internet and ran across some heckler blacklisting a well-known (and well-loved) pastor because the pastor dared to say that God wants to speak to us. But it's true: we can hear God.

This heart-conversation, this hearing of God's voice, feels like such a big responsibility when we think it's up to us. But the burden doesn't fall on our ability to hear as much as it does God's ability to speak. And he does speak. Our job is to listen.

Let's consider some of the more common ways we can listen:

1. **God speaks through his Word** (Josh. 1:8; Ps. 119).
   If we believe the Bible as God's own words with man as the mere messenger, then when we read it, we hear God speak in very real and practical ways.[26]

   Ever want to know what God's thinking about a particular topic? He's already laid it out for us, like a reference manual. If we spend dedicated time in his Word, we come to know and understand his voice. The Bible also serves as an ongoing plumb line for the other avenues God may use to speak to us—his voice will never contradict his Word.

2. **God speaks through others** (Eph. 4:12; 1 Cor. 12:27).
   We have to pay attention to the conversations around us.

   God has used friends, authors, and speakers, books, songs, and movies to speak very specifically into my personal situations. God sometimes places people in our paths who will confirm his plans for us—they may do this with a simple word of encouragement that sparks agreement within our spirits, or confirming words that repeat what the Lord has already placed within us.

3. **God speaks through prayer** (Jer. 33:3; Matt. 21:22).
   When we sit quietly with the Lord, there is often a gentle prompting in our thoughts that leads and directs us into his ways.

   Too many of us turn to God just so we can feel better, telling him what bothers us, what we want and think we need, and then we leave. But prayer is a two-way thing, an actual conversation. God wants us to listen for his everyday input—not just turn to him in times of crisis.[27]

4. **God speaks through circumstances** (Rom. 8:28).
   If we examine a little more closely those life events that appear mere coincidences, we may be surprised to discover God's intervention.

Ever have a set of events line up in an uncanny way? Amazing coincidences rarely "fall" into place, no matter how it appears. When we look closer, we usually see how God is the only One that could have orchestrated those events. *Providence, not coincidence.* Even in bad circumstances like illness or financial ruin or the many other things that strike, we have to trust God is somehow working. While I'm not suggesting that God brings bad things into our lives to prove a point, I do believe God can and does work through our circumstances, good and bad. These are the times we must cling to his sovereignty.

5. **God speaks through the Words of his Son** (Heb. 1:1–2; John 1:14–18).
   Jesus is a direct expression of God's heart—when Jesus speaks, we can hear God.

   Jesus "is the radiance of the glory of God and the exact imprint of his nature."[28] Jesus came to demonstrate God's love. Through Jesus, we can know what God is like, his very heart, and what he has to say.

6. **God speaks through sneak previews** (Rom. 1:20; Ps. 19:1–4).
   There's something about the glory of God radiating throughout creation that tests the temperature of our hearts, that says, "I am here," if you're willing to see me.

   Gentle, sashaying bodies of river water irrigate the southeastern region where I live; our community depends on it. But these rivers are powerful, picking up tremendous force as they feed into larger bodies of water. As I watch them, I sense God saying, "I am here." How can we look at the handiwork of God's masterpiece and not get a glimpse of his character, a whisper of his passion, power, and wisdom?

The Power of an Intentional Pause

The shrill of the kitchen phone cut through my sleep—an unwelcome intrusion for the late morning sleep-in I had planned.

I scrunched the covers snugly around my neck, turning on my right side. The digital clock glared 7:09 A.M. My thoughts panned to the day ahead while the warmth of my fleece blanket tempted my sleepy eyes.

I glanced at the cell phone sitting on my night stand. *Five missed calls?* Quickly, I dialed voicemail.

"Tabitha's been in a wreck." Her boyfriend's voice cracked.

The mound of blankets fell to my ankles as I whirled out of bed. I grabbed my jeans while listening to the rest of the message. "Some woman called me," he said. "Tabitha's head is bleeding. They're taking her to The Medical Center."

One hand pulling up my jeans, I fumbled to retrieve the next message.

"This is Brian," Tabitha's half-brother said. "I was on my way to work. There's a bad wreck on the interstate. Not much left of the car . . . ," he cleared his throat. "But there's a custom orange stripe down the side. Just like Tabitha's. It doesn't look good, Jo Ann."

This can't be possible. Surely there's some mistake.

I jumped in my car and headed toward the hospital. A mere ten minutes away, an easy drive from my house. Fighting nausea, I gripped the steering wheel with trembling hands and tried to focus. *This is not happening.*

About twenty minutes later, I pulled my car up to a strange intersection. I was lost—in my own hometown. Tears clouded my vision until I felt pressed to simply sit still. *God, where am I? Where are you?*

I realized I had failed to listen to the remaining messages on my voicemail. As I turned the car around, I grabbed my phone and pressed some buttons.

"Jo Ann, this is Brian." I heard the caller say. "I'm in the room with Tabitha and she's going to be fine. She's going to be okay."

Thank you, God.

The mental fog lifted. I'd driven in circles; the hospital was directly behind me. I'd turned a short ten-minute drive into a twenty-minute nightmare.

In the waiting room I spotted Tabitha's boyfriend first, then her brother Brian.

"They asked us to wait here." Brian said.

I pushed through the emergency doors and faced an endless maze of hallways. I chose a left turn that landed me in front of a tall, fair-skinned man, pushing someone on a stretcher—it was Tabitha. Ashen-faced, with blood oozing out of her scalp and multiple bruises covering her thin body—I barely recognized her.

Wide-eyed and bordering panic, we locked eyes. "Mama," she cried. "Am I going to die?"

Something lifted my fears, spoke words I didn't feel. "No, honey, you're going to be okay—you're going to be just fine."

The attendant turned the stretcher toward trauma room 3. Partitioned by sliding curtains, the room was small. Two men lifted Tabitha from the backboard onto a steel table, scantily covered with a thin pad and white sheet. Bright lights streamed overhead. Plastic apparatus, oxygen tanks, and digital monitors hung from the wall.

"Where's the neurologist?" someone called out. The skilled hands of multiple nurses and a physician responded quickly to Tabitha's many symptoms. Minutes seemed eternal.

About a half hour later, the emergency physician turned to me, "We have to get her head sewn up. She's taken quite a hit. We're going to have to watch her for neurological damage, but I think she's going to be alright—after a long recovery, anyway."

Brian and Tabitha's boyfriend joined us outside of her room. "Is she going to be okay?" Brian asked, peeking in on her.

"I think so," I said. "I'm just thankful you were able to get in here when she first arrived. I was so panicked I couldn't even find my way here until I got your voicemail that said she was going to be alright."

Brian frowned. "This is the first time I've seen her, Jo Ann. We had to wait outside the whole time. They wouldn't let us back here."

Pulling back the curtain, the physician walked through. "She's all sewn up. We'll transfer her over to ICU so we can keep a close watch on her neurological responses." He stepped aside.

Everyone pushed in to check on Tabitha, but I drew back. Confused, I dialed my voicemail again. Oddly, the comforting message from Brian—the one telling me he was in the room with Tabitha, and that she was going to be okay—was missing.

Seven years later, I still have no explanation for that experience. But I do know when I sat lost at that intersection I felt a prompting to simply be still. And in the stillness, I was pressed to check my voicemails.

Sometimes we're so desperate to hear God speak to us that when he does, we discount it.

Think back again to David. Before he was a king, he was a shepherd. A shepherd who understood how quietness often elicits a Word from God. In the psalms, David frequently used the term "Selah." Commonly understood as a technical musical term, Selah expressed the need for a pause, a rest.

David often cried out from the depths of his heart, and God, in his grace, answered. Then, there was an intentional pause. As if God were saying, "Be still. Let's just sit with this for a little while."

I suspect David went on many such heart-journeys, where he sat with God in a quiet silence that carried him to this holy confrontation. An interval of silence with a sovereign God. A reflective moment to contemplate fresh revelation. These moments of opportunity, they hold tremendous power for lasting change.

Selah-moments: those times we lean into God's presence, hear his voice, and willingly receive the golden nuggets of truth-revelation he gifts us with.

That Day God's Voice Leads Us to Our Own

Long ago, Jesus set a precedent for the value of a woman's voice. In a time when women's words didn't count for much, he intentionally (sometimes scandalously) pursued those who were hurt and rejected, choosing to love and respect them, proving their value and worth to onlookers. Jesus would go out of his way to reach these silenced and ignored ones, guiding them into God's plan. He does the same for us still.

In John 4, we have a powerful example in the Samaritan woman. Beware of a familiarity that urges you to discount this story, because it effectively demonstrates the power of a hurting woman's voice to inspire people beyond her lifetime.

This is how I imagine it all played out—this woman finding her voice.

We find the Pharisees upset, rumbling and mumbling over all the disciple-making and baptizing going on. Hostility was growing toward Jesus, though, ironically, it wasn't even him doing the baptizing.

What did Jesus do? What we feel like doing most days—he packed his bags and left town.

As Jesus left Judea and traveled north to Galilee, he passed through Samaria. Interestingly, this was not the only route—it was actually the less-traveled one. According to the Reformation Study Bible, the Jews hated the Samaritan people so much that the Jews would cross the river twice rather than pass through Samaria.[29] They considered the Samaritans impure because of their inter-marriages with pagan tribes, feeling there was nothing worse than turning your back on fellow Israelites and God.

But God had a plan, and Jesus had a divine date with a five-times-divorced, brokenhearted woman. He and his disciples headed to Sychar, a small mountain town that sat on the west side of the Jordan River between Judea and Galilee.

Hot, tired, and thirsty, they made their way straight to the town's watering hole. A well that the patriarch Jacob had long ago built still served as the source of water for local folks and weary travelers. After the disciples dropped Jesus off at the well, they headed into town to grab some food.

In the heat of the day, Jesus sat on the edge of the well—glad for the break. Soon a Samaritan woman came to get her daily water.

Now, most women did this chore in the cooler part of day to avoid the sweltering sun—makes me think our nameless friend didn't want to run into anyone. Makes sense when you consider she'd been divorced five times, and divorce was not looked upon favorably, especially for a woman.

Here's the thing: regardless of blame, this woman had been through *five* divorces. I've been divorced; I know the pain. We're talking five divorces. I imagine she barely got distanced from one divorce before facing another. Tell me this woman wasn't hurting emotionally.

So here comes soul-wounded "Sam" to draw her water in the heat of the day in order to avoid the disapproving looks of other women. And a stranger—a Jewish stranger—speaks to her. Talk about a cultural taboo. Some Jewish men didn't even speak to their wives or mothers in public and here was Jesus talking to a woman, a Samaritan woman at that.

"Will you give me something to drink?" Jesus asked.

A man—a Jew—speaking to me? In the middle of day, in the middle of town? And he's not angry? I wonder if he plans to take advantage of me like most men have.

To quickly earn her trust, I suspect Jesus appealed to the natural nurturer in her by asking for help. Who among us doesn't feel the tug of someone in need?

Puzzled but intrigued, Sam felt pressed to speak—maybe even with a slight edge to her voice, "How come you, a Jew, are asking me, a Samaritan woman, for a drink?"[30]

Who Doesn't Love a Free Gift

"If you knew the gift of God, and who it is that is saying to you, 'Give me a drink,' you would have asked him, and he would have given you living water," Jesus said.

Why is this man talking to me? And why am I drawn to respond? All I wanted was water—but this?

Jesus uses a distinct Greek word for gift here—*dorea*, which means a free gift.[31] Again, Jesus knows how to reach a girl's heart. What woman refuses a gift? A free gift.

To draw water, you have to prime the pump, right? Instead of priming the pump for her well water, Sam found herself primed by Jesus with an offer of divine Dasani. I don't know that she fully comprehends what he's offering, but she's certainly captivated.

"Give me that water."

Not so fast. Jesus knew she wasn't quite ready. He had to dig a little further by piercing her personal problems with truth, exposing her heart.

Healing begins at truth-telling.

"Go get your husband," he said.

"But I don't have one," she responded.

"That's certainly the truth. You're currently living with a man and you've had five failed marriages before this relationship."

Ouch.

How could he know such intimate details? He's new in town, hasn't even had time to be subjected to the town gossip. Surely this man is a prophet.

Like a lot of women in her town, Sam believed in the coming of Jesus—a Messiah who would reveal *all* to them, give them the whole story. I can't help but wonder if at this point she's thinking, maybe, just maybe, this is him—this man who can tell me the things I've done.

Some time must have passed because, while they are still talking, Jesus' disciples returned with the groceries. And they were pretty surprised to see Jesus talking to a woman. It was bad enough he'd carried them through a town they probably never wanted to step foot in, but now Jesus stands, in the middle of the day in the town center, openly chatting with a Samaritan. And a woman.

After her talk with Jesus, Sam was so enamored, so changed, that she forgot what she came there for. Dropping the water jar, she bolted off to meet the same townsfolk she normally avoided. (Now that's when you know Jesus has changed you—when you leave everything behind to return to the very people who ridiculed and rejected you, so you can share his love.)

"Come see a man who told me all that I ever did. Could this be the Christ?"

All. I. Ever. Did.

Whether Sam was prone to embellish or not, I don't know. But can you imagine what *all* Jesus told her to make her feel like everything dishonorable she'd ever done had been revealed? She and Jesus talked at length but the most we hear about are the five husbands and the current living arrangements. I suspect there's much more than that.

I hope it doesn't take Jesus recounting everything we've ever done before we're willing to listen to his voice, to hear his truth. But may we be open to it if that *is* what it takes. After all, it was Sam's public confession that drew in countless people to Jesus.

"Her confession regarding the exposure of her past was probably so explicit and beyond the realm of fabrication that she became a compelling advocate. . . . This woman's testimony was so powerful that it transcended the cultural barriers."[32]

With a pierced heart, yet emotionally free, the Samaritan woman was no longer silenced. The woman at the well—a nameless ordinary woman who had endured such pain and ridicule became a powerful mouthpiece for Jesus; some even called her the "first woman evangelist."

We ourselves get to witness an entire town's transformation because of her voice. A voice she uncovered by responding to the voice of God.

Amazing what a simple conversation
with Jesus can do.

God's Healing Words

Precious daughter,

You are safe to leave your water jar, safe to turn to me for all your needs. Yes, all of your needs. I really do love you. And I really do have great plans for you.

I long to share those plans with you but I cannot unless you can hear me and follow me. If you come to me with an expectant and listening attitude, if you sit in regular conversation with me, I will speak to you.

You must learn to be still, to wait on my voice, my truth that will fill your thirsty heart.

Remember the first time you heard my voice? That sensing of my presence, that heart-stirring that brought you into an intimate covenant relationship with me? Hearing me today is still that way—pay attention to that familiarity. Practice spending time with me.

I have your best interests at heart, here. Will you listen? Really listen? The more you choose to listen to me, the easier it becomes.

Will you start believing me—not just believe in me, but believe me? Will you trust me? One day, you will have my character and my love for you so etched in your mind that you will know to trust my voice. Until then, keep practicing my voice based on the Words I've left you in Scripture.

I'm always here for you. There won't be one time that you turn to me and I'm not. Choose today to walk under the covering of my safe, protective love. The same love that will walk into your future with you.

As you learn to recognize my voice, you will uncover yours—a voice directly tied to your identity and purpose, to my plans for you. Don't be anxious over the next step, my plan will unfold as we go. Simply trust for now. Just listen for my voice. It's the one laced in truth, love, hope, and joy. The One that draws you into me, into my safe and loving arms. The One that leads you home.

Love,

The Voice of Truth

THE VOICE STUDIO:

Responding to God's Call to Develop Our Voices

Hearing the Voice of God

1. Do you recognize the voice of God? In what ways does he speak to you? How does he guide you?
2. Describe the first time you "heard" God. Are you regularly hearing from God now? What do you feel blocks you from clearly hearing him?
3. How can prayer train you to hear God's voice?
4. Do you allow yourself to be or even stay angry at God? Does that affect your ability to trust him? To hear him?
5. What was the last thing God pressed onto your heart, prompted you to do? Have you ever ignored a prompting from God—talked yourself out of it? Why? What was the result?
6. Do you ever feel like God is silent? How do you respond to that? What do you wish God would say to you?
7. What story do you hold that has the potential to influence others, like the Samaritan woman who changed an entire community with her words?
8. Has anyone ever said something to you that felt like the exact answer you were seeking? How did that make you feel? Did you act on it?

9. What is your "point of doubt"? What promises does God offer that you simply can't believe or receive?

10. How can you tell the difference between your voice, God's voice, and the Enemy's voice?

A Purpose for the Pain

The Journey to a Stronger, More Realistic Faith

That thing that you want to hide is the very thing God wants to use.
~Steven Furtick

"God, you've turned your back on me." Alice said. "An infection killed my son—it wasn't even the cancer that killed him. You could have prevented that. Why didn't you do something?"

The selfish chill of the February night pierced Alice Wisler's heart. She cradled her son, four-year-old Daniel, as he sucked in his last breath. After eight months of chemo, radiation, and surgeries targeting the neuroblastoma in his neck, Daniel's weakened body failed the surprise attack of a staph infection.

Daniel—the boy "whose smile was as bright as the sun over a Carolina beach, the boy who friended ladybugs and toads and liked telling jokes he'd memorized from a worn-out joke book, the boy whose only enemy was the cancer inside his little body"—was gone.[33]

"This is it for us, God." Alice said. "You can stay over there. And I'll be over here. That's just the way it's going to have to be—there's no way I can ever trust you again. Somehow I will have to adapt to life without Daniel, but it will also be without you."

The Unique Education Such Pain Brings

Alice's hand landed on a plaid-covered journal. *This is perfect. I can write about the children's first visit to my homeland.*

A missionary kid from Japan, Alice was excited about the plans she and her husband had with young Daniel, his older sister Rachel, and baby brother Benjamin, to head to Hawaii and then on to Japan—until Daniel's diagnosis ambushed those plans.

Instead of adventure and exciting travels, the family moved to the hospital one week of each month for chemo infusions. It was here Alice salvaged the journal as it became a source of hope while she filled the crisp pages with recorded prayers and fresh dreams for Daniel's future.

When someone relieved her from Daniel's bedside, Alice headed straight to the coffee shop to write. To pray. To believe. *God, I trust that you're going to heal Daniel of this aggressive tumor.*

Alice never expected the outcome to be Daniel's death. *How do you pit a good God against something so unfair?*

Three months after Daniel died, Alice gave birth to her fourth child. Nursing a newborn, coddling an eighteen-month-old, and nurturing a six-year-old, Alice's heartache eventually overtook her.

"I'm the mom of a son who died," she said. "My four-year-old died—and I'm supposed to live without him? Take me too, Death. I can't do this."

Alice turned to a new journal, a cloth-bound book with blue-and-red-swirled flowers on the front—a gift from the oncology nurse. But this journal no longer held hope-filled prayers. Instead it was filled with anger, sorrow, and questions. Lots of questions.

Each day, while her husband managed the children for a short reprieve, Alice headed off to the rounded, drooping branches of a weeping willow tree in a close-by park.

"As I went through the motions of the day, I knew there was going to be a time at the end of the day where I could just go and write. I could get stuff out that was bottled up inside me. Writing became a really close friend. Although I was numb, I stumbled through the day knowing I would soon be able to release my real feelings."

That sheer anticipation fostered Alice's healing, an honest recounting of her pain delivering an unusual perspective. "While I often hated having a reason to have to write, I will always be grateful that my writing was there for me—never judgmental, never belittling, never preachy."

Alice's loss cultivated a common connection with other hurting women. Sixteen years after Daniel's death, she is an award-winning author and speaker who shares from her new reality—one without Daniel. In his memory, Alice founded Daniel's House Publications, a grief organization. She now travels the country speaking, teaching, and reaching out to others who have lost a child to death.

"We often think it's all about us—how much we suffer, how much we cry, how tormented we feel," Alice said. "But when we weigh all of our misery against God's grace, grace outweighs it all. His compassion is stronger, fiercer than our struggle; his love more constant, radiant, and healing, than any problem in our den of lions."[34]

Sometimes a stronger, more realistic faith
is birthed in the darkest of pits.

Why We Really Can Live without Knowing Why

Theologians and diverse scholars offer assorted and sometimes contradictory explanations on why bad things happen to people. I won't stir the mix with my spiritual ignorance; I sure don't have life figured out.

I've wasted valuable time, crossed off too many days, searching the *why* answers. Like the disciples who asked Jesus about a man who was blind from birth, I needed someone to blame but there was no blame to attach.[35]

If we blame God, if we get stuck in the "why" of it all,
we tempt a hard-heartedness that can
soil our hearts.

One day Jesus and his disciples were walking down the street and ran into a blind man. The disciples wanted to know why the man was blind. "Whose sin caused this?" they asked.

Isn't that just like us? *Whose fault is this? Who can we pin this on?* Determined to understand, we demand explanations.

But Jesus said, "You're asking the wrong question. You're looking for someone to blame. . . . Look instead for what God can do."[36]

Look for what God can do. What a fresh perspective. Are we willing to consider some of life's circumstances as ready-made opportunities for God to be displayed in and through us? We may never understand the why. Sometimes God answers us, sometimes he doesn't. But we really can live without knowing.

Because if we cooperate with God, if we fully surrender our hurts to him, he will somehow use every ounce of pain we've ever walked through. No matter the depth of our hurts, we cannot ignore God's incredible love and power that ultimately takes everything that happens in our lives and transforms it into something good. If we love him, if we keep our eyes on him, it all works out. He promises.

Allow me a shadow of caution here? As I walk alongside broken-hearted women daily, I'm careful about the use of Romans 8:28. It's hard to tell someone who just lost a family member to a random act of violence, or the mother of three children whose husband just walked out, that "in all things God works for the good of those who love him" (NIV).

Too often this verse serves as an insipid, overused Christian cliché for some who are either afraid or ill-equipped to address some tough issues.

Frequently, we quote that verse without the beginning words, three key words: "And we know." We must *know.* We must be confident God is working, even in this. Even when nothing makes sense. That type of confidence alters a perspective, frees you from old ways of thinking.

That knowing comes in time, but until then we find our sanity and strength in a God that guides us through these hard places.

Look for what God can do. In the end, Jesus healed the blind man so well that he was unrecognizable. "Is this even the same man?" some asked.

Jesus can heal our hurts with such a complete wholeness that people won't even know we were ever wounded. "Every detail . . . worked into something good," as only God can do. And that becomes much more important than an explanation why something happened in the first place.[37]

Want to sample some real freedom right now? Speak this life-transforming truth aloud, then repeat as needed: *I don't know why—I may never know why, and that's okay with me.*

There is a powerful shifting that takes place
as we abandon the right to understand
and we yield to God's working in our lives.

Here's another deliciously irresistible taste of freedom. What if instead of asking "Why?" we started asking "What's next?" This question alone has the potential to change our lives.

Are we that afraid of surrender
that we would choose our current discontent or misery
over what God has in store?

But This Wasn't Supposed to Happen

Girl-to-girl here? Even now, I'm in a place where I'm having to abandon this right to understand, and instead "look for what God can do." And there are honestly times when I wonder if it hurts more to push through the day or to watch another night fall.

I'm in a unique season. A season of helping one precious to me while my own desires and dreams suspend mid-air. Days of rising (way) too early, cleaning behind little ears, and finding fun learning activities to entertain a hungry young mind—all while cloaking discipleship in the painting of rocks and baking of cookies.

Even with Jesus, it sounds as ridiculous to me as the pursuit sometimes feels. *I'm not this selfless.*

I'm a Nana, and a writer with lofty dreams, yet my days are spent hands-on parenting my granddaughter while praying healing prayers for my own girl. Late at night I drop exhausted, but not before addressing mounds of laundry, piled high like seconds of last night's whipped potatoes. (Why does everything make me want to eat nowadays?)

My self-care tapers to popping Lil Critters Gummy Vites and Omega 3s after wrestling Rapunzel for tub space. Meanwhile the days pass, evaporating like the water in yesterday's forgotten pan—boiling dry, flooding the air for mere moments.

There's nothing like a return to mothering to reduce you to the basics. *Breathe in. Breathe out.*

And then there are those days that the invisible illness taunts. Hips that scream in neuropathic pain, hands and legs that won't always cooperate, thought processes that dim.

Normally, I share this (the depth of my emotional and physical pain) with a limited few. I don't often voice it with new friends, for I fear that in their compassion they may somehow side with that ugly shoot of righteousness that tempts some days to push right through. They've done it before, applauded my actions—courageous and charitable some call it. If they only knew how self–focus and the mere idea of sacrifice cuts a fresh trail of pride in my heart.

Truth is, it's often too much for me on my own. It's solely God's grace in action, this crushing of self. It's only him that instills in me any inkling of service, forcing me to lean into him completely as he teaches me to trust.

Isn't it funny how God teaches us his ways by sometimes starting with what we lack the most?

The realization brings a smile. Long ago, I told Jesus I want to be where he is—nowhere else; the desire blooming not from a spiritual maturity but rather a tiredness of making such horrific mistakes when left to myself to choose. *This*, these long days and longer nights, this *is* where he is working.

There are those lessons you learn only through sacrifice,
like how the wounds of a loved one's
heart can heal
when you give God room to work.

When you're willing to step into the uncomfortable, willing to help when you feel you cannot, willing to trust your unanswered questions to a God who knows, who cares—those are the sort of real-life actions that make a place for God to move.

Those days, those nights I feel I can't continue? Somehow God *is* working—even in this.

What if the aches,
they are somehow equipping me
for what's next?

What if those are the precise moments that propel me to lean in, allow him to carry me? And these dreams of mine, will they not produce the greater harvest after being germinated in God's own hand?

We've talked about this; how this change of thinking is a process and not a quick fix. So for now, I'm applying these same principles that I share with you, the ones I've seen work for me right when I'm in the middle of the mess.

Meanwhile, I'm learning to love more (God's way) while creating special memories for use in later years. And besides, this extra stress is a great way to justify those extra servings of mashed potatoes as the "serotonin surge" I need just to keep up (stay sane).

The Divine Move into Greater Priorities

"It's an especially severe form of neck and tongue cancer. Stage 4." Dr. Line said to Misty. "Your husband's chances are almost nonexistent."

Misty and her husband, Joe, were former Hollywood glam. Joe was a seasoned actor, having appeared on *Days of Our Lives*, *General Hospital*, and *Three's Company*. Misty was an accomplished screenwriter, one of the very first women to ever write for animation in Hollywood. Personally mentored by William Hanna (Hanna Barbera Productions), Misty had written not only for *Scooby-Doo*, but also for shows like *Knots Landing*, *Fantasy Island*, *Incredible Hulk*, and others.

But the lights of Hollywood couldn't help them now. Misty needed a lifeline—her always healthy, wonderfully supportive husband (and best friend) was facing death. She did the only thing she knew to do: she turned to God.

"I love you, God, but I don't understand you. What you've done is mean. I want to say I know this is covered by your plan, but when your loved one is lying there, suffering with invasive tubes in every orifice, it's hard. I need you. Here. Now."

"I'm right here, Misty. Will you trust me with this?" she felt God impress on her heart.

Hours barely passed until the battle for Joe was in full swing. Misty already had a professional relationship with Dr. Line, the specialist who discovered Joe's cancer. He was the same doctor who had treated her allergies years before she was even married to Joe. Dr. Line got things rolling the minute the tests came in; not a second was lost. They saw all the right people. Started treatment immediately. And, in the end, saved Joe's life.

You thought I wasn't there, and I was. You were angry. You were afraid. And that was okay—I loved you through it. Journaling the words she felt God press on her heart reminded Misty (reminds us all) we can't always know what God is up to, but we can learn to trust and believe him.

Ever wonder why God doesn't intervene—
why he doesn't just behave the way we think he should?

I don't know why Misty and Joe had to go through that, but I know that when Joe was healed, folks were watching and God received the glory. Just like when he healed Lazarus, Jesus never bothered explaining the why to Mary and Martha beforehand.[38] From our vantage point, we understood the death was for God's glory, so that people would believe in Jesus. But what did those girls have to go on in the middle of the crisis?

Ancient tradition believed the soul hovered near the body of a dead person for three days with the possibility of returning, but on the fourth day the person was truly dead. Whether the belief was true was irrelevant, had Jesus returned prematurely, doubters would discount his miracle.

"Didn't I tell you if you believe that you will see the glory of God?" Jesus looked Mary in the eye.[39]

Those painful things we didn't want to happen, those hard places we didn't want to be—how it often takes a direct look from God for us to remember that he's still with us. And somehow, often unexplainable to us, we and others watching will see his glory in all of this.

That more genuine faith we've talked about? We step into that when we accept that the hurts of our past aren't nearly as important as what God wants to do with our future. As Mark Buchanan says in *The Rest of God*, "What *will* happen matters more than what *has* happened."[40]

Dare we look beyond the pain?

For a long time, God and I had this sterile I-have-to-do-everything-right-lest-he-drop-his-hammer-of-justice-all-over-me kind of thing going on. You can probably sense that from some of my earlier journal entries. But after a decade of trying to live out this skewed perspective of Christianity, I finally realized that wasn't what God wanted at all.

But there were a couple of things that were pretty important to him.

One, God simply wanted an intimate love-relationship with me. He wanted a committed heart-to-heart relationship. He loves me as his child. I love him as my Father. We talk; he tells me what he's thinking, I tell him what I'm thinking, we both listen. And we have a strong relationship, rooted in love and respect.

Two, God's ultimate desire for my life is to bring him glory, to live in a way that others would see his greatness in spite of anything, good or bad, that enters or leaves my life. While it goes against everything about our brokenness, God has instilled in us the power to interpret life differently, to gain a new perspective in spite of what's happened to us, and the power to respond to him differently from this new place of truth.

Like Misty and Joe facing that illness, like Mary, Martha, and Lazarus going through their family crisis, my ultimate purpose is to somehow bring honor to him.[41]

So how do we,
hurting hearts in tow,
honor God with our lives?

Moving from Blame to Action

I'm not asking you to deny reality, to push back a pain as if it never existed. I wouldn't dare. Others have pressed me to do such a thing and I know the searing guilt that such an assumption brings. I am, however, asking you to reconsider what has happened in the context of a much bigger story.

Sometimes we have to let God change the way we see things. Paul calls it "being transformed by the renewing of our minds."[42] It isn't easy—a bit unnatural actually. But it is possible.

We have mentors who modeled this for us, this change of perspective. Mary, the mother of Jesus, was a young unwed mother surrounded by stares of shameful disgrace, but she saw Jesus. King David saw things from a unique perspective, too. Others saw some mammoth warrior, Goliath; David saw God.

It isn't what we see
as much as it is how we see it.

In his book, *To Be Told*, Dan Allender invites us to re-engage the tragedies of our lives from a different perspective. "While we can't change our life events, or eliminate the people who have played a role in our life story, we can write a new plot, a new story line, if we re-engage these tragedies with new patterns of thought."[43]

There's a sixth-century prophet named Haggai who arouses that same optimism within us.

In one of the shortest books of the Bible, which bears this prophet's name, we uncover a man who outlasted the Babylonian exile. Here is someone who understood oppression, profound discouragement, and the pain of yesterday, but chose instead to set his eyes on the future.

Understanding the importance of right perspective, Haggai often challenged those around him to look at things from this same angle—this forward-focus.

Desolate times peppered the second year of King Darius's reign. Under his leadership, the exiles had grown restless and discontented. Following God's plan wasn't as much fun as it used to be, not the priority it once was for the Jewish people. Years earlier, God had instructed them to rebuild the temple that was burned, leveled to the ground during their captivity. But so far, all they built was a solid wall of excuses. Now that they were free, they were more intent on rebuilding their own homes and restoring the devastation of earlier years.

Will our brokenness steer us into a place
of privilege with God,
one where his very breath whispers
healing and purpose,
or will it lead us into a dangerous sense of entitlement
that poisons God's plans?

You can't really blame the captives, after all they'd been through. I probably would have been stomping my feet, demanding a little "me" time myself. But there were a few hard truths that were in play here.

1. God's assigned work is always the greatest priority (no matter our feelings about what is happening or what has happened).
2. Getting what we want isn't always what we need.
3. God doesn't owe us anything.

The hurts of life should never cause us to put off, or worse, abandon, what we know God wants us to do. While God is loving and compassionate, he knows what we need better than we do. And those times we take a wrong turn, he will usually send someone to call us out, much like Haggai did with the Jewish people: "Take a good, hard look at your life. Think it over."[44]

But those burdened with life's demands can't always see clearly. "It's not time," they said. "We aren't ready."

How often those same thoughts
steer us away from a work
God longs to do in us.

God knew they would never be ready if left to themselves, so he pressed them for a change of perspective. "Who of you remembers what *I* want to do?" God asked them (and us). "Don't you remember my promise? I am still with you. Don't be afraid of what we're about to go through. It's worth it. . . . Take courage, for I am with you."[45]

God offers us the same promise of peace and restoration that he offered the Jewish captives who were willing to do the hard work. Greater things than the life of our past await us. The later years will be greater than the early years. He promises.

Like a silversmith who transforms badly tarnished silver into gleaming works of beauty, God hand polishes our pain. He carefully massages the tarnished areas and scrubs any caked-on residue until it disappears into a beautiful shine, a shine that reflects his image.

That shine? *That* is when a hurting woman honors God with her life.

Why We Must Repeat Truth until We Believe

"Syringo-my-what?" On guard, forty-two-year-old Jean Kinsey faced the neurosurgeon.

"Syringomyelia—a very rare disease." The surgeon's eyes softened. "There's a syrinx, a fluid-filled cyst, in your spinal cord and it's growing toward your brain. You need immediate surgery. Without it, you can only expect to live a couple more months."

A chronic disorder, syringomyelia, known as SM, had formed this life-threatening cyst, hinting at its presence with numbness and electrical sensations sprinkled throughout Jean's body over the past few weeks. The avid walker, bowler, and dedicated mom had been only mildly concerned about the unusual symptoms.

"What about my children?" Jean turned toward the surgeon's hand on her shoulder. "My husband doesn't go to church—my children need me!"

When the storm hits, you search for something to hold you in place.

Jean battled mounting insecurities, fears, and doubts that mustered the night before surgery. It was here she remembered God's promises, anchoring herself with one from Psalm 23. *I may walk through valleys as dark as death, but I won't be afraid. You are with me.*[46] She recited it over and over—until she believed it. *Walking through the valley. Won't be afraid. You are with me.* Eventually, she drifted off into a peaceful sleep.

Recovery was intense and long. With limited movement, she was forced to develop new life skills while the financial strain of a prolonged illness exhausted her family.

When her legs failed, Jean sewed and made crafts—making all the children's clothing. That is, until her hands became as useless as her legs.

"God, I'm trying not to question your will—I know you must have a plan." Jean said. "But this hurts."

Jean knew how to get through tough times. In preparation, God had blessed her with an influential grandmother who modeled thankfulness in the face of adversity. Wed to a drunkard husband with no ambition, Jean's grandmother was forced to provide for her six children alone. But Jean never heard a complaint, only gratitude.

"Thank you, God, for the oil we have in our lamps." Each night, her grandmother maintained an attitude of thankfulness, even as she lit the household lamps that stood in the shadow of her neighbor's electricity.

With Jean's church praying for a miracle (something she had never really entertained), she resolved to accept her crisis with the very grace her grandmother modeled. With Psalms as her yardstick, Jean returned to God to seek guidance and strength.

"Help me dwell on the positive, Lord, not the negative. Help me to be thankful for the little oil I have in my lamps and the abundance of love you have for me," Jean said.

After coming to grips with her disability, Jean starting writing for *Faces*, a monthly support paper for others with SM, produced by the American Syringomyelia Alliance Project. The profiles of individuals with SM encouraged Jean and others across the country.

Saddled in the grief of her losses, Jean could have been crippled—figuratively and literally. But a willingness to consider another perspective afforded her great new adventures as she made a conscious decision to write a new story line.

"There will always be a pain and a yearning for what I've lost, but I don't dwell on it," Jean said.

A miracle came after all. Because of the nerve damage, most people with SM totally lose mobility as the disease progresses. However, Jean continues to be blessed with some mobility after twenty-five years of living with the disease. But she admits the real miracle is the peace God planted within her, in spite of such a debilitating illness, and that God allows her to share this peace with others through the craft of writing. With the free time Jean's illness allows, she now spends several hours a day writing novels and inspirational material, ministering to others through stories published in various anthologies and periodicals.

When We Allow God to Do with Us as He Wishes

I don't want to live one more day like this, Lord. I can't.

One day I snuggled up nice and close to the thick depression that had been hanging around. She'd patiently waited for the day my heart would be stretched so thin that I would fling the door open, welcome her company. Unsure when things had gotten so hard, I nestled my brokenness into her ready arms. We drew close as she brought out the photos, the flashbacks and hard memories of things I'd never wanted to see.

I imagine some lessons can only be learned in the dark.

God knew I needed one of those "direct looks." The look that says, "I know this seems messy, but I've got a plan."

An enticing strength tempted my depressive fog with a straightforward question, a question attempting to claw right through my black empty. "Will you consider a long-term view of your suffering?"

A long-term view? You mean a get-my-eyes-off-myself-somehow view? You do remember how much I've been hurt, right?

Philip Yancey, in *Where Is God When It Hurts*, says it like this: "The important issue facing Christians who suffer is not 'Is God responsible?' but 'How should I react now that this terrible thing has happened?'"

Is there hope that these hurts of life harbor some sort of long-term sustenance, a framework for God's grace–plan somehow? Throughout the scriptures, God reveals a much bigger story than we can begin to comprehend. Could these hurts be a piece of that, somehow fitting into a larger story?

Could our lives be providentially connected with others? What if we could somehow move beyond our own losses by investing in the lives of others who have experienced similar pains? Could the sharing of these common pains allow a heart–connection otherwise unattainable?

The truth, like an unexpected and much-needed spring rain, washed over my eyes: my suffering, our suffering, matters.

Dr. Katie Brazelton, founder of Life Purpose Coaching Centers, International®, has been an influential mentor in my life, encouraging me to move beyond the pain of my past, to press forward, trusting God's purposes for my life. To allow the purpose of the hurts I've walked through to become much more important than the cause.

> God's pleasure is to make good out of bad. He is your loving and generous Father. He has a way of delicately wrapping all the parts of your life together as a package deal to give you hope and purpose. Whether tragedy has torn up your life . . . all that matters now is that you decide to allow God to do with you as he wishes. Trust that he will use the best and worst of your past [and present too] to fulfill his purposes for your life.[47]

Katie also introduced me to the work of Viktor Frankl. Between 1942 and 1945, Frankl spent time in four different Nazi concentration camps. As an inmate, he spent those years enduring atrocious suffering, and watching others suffer. The following year he wrote a book about those experiences, *Man's Search for Meaning*, concluding that life *always* has meaning and purpose, even in the throes of intense suffering. Strange how such a hard book (and experience) laced with death and radical evil could hold hope, but such was his perspective.

> We who lived in the concentration camps can remember the men who walked through the huts comforting others, giving away their last piece of bread. They may have been few in number, but they offer sufficient proof that everything can be taken from a man but one thing: the last of the human freedoms—to choose one's attitude in any given set of circumstances, to choose one's own way. . . . In some way, suffering ceases to be suffering at the moment it finds a meaning.[48]

Raising High the White Flag

When does the emotional suffering end? When we find meaning.

When do we find meaning? At the point of total surrender to God.

Surrender. Perhaps the word rolls off the tongue a little distastefully? Relinquishing control is hard for those who lived so much of our lives out of control. I wonder if, like me, you've fearfully micro-managed your life—spent years trying to simultaneously live this life of surrender and control.

I used to think surrendering to God meant I would reach some mystical point where I no longer cared what had happened to me, what was currently happening, or even what my future held. To surrender meant the bad things that happened in life were okay.

They weren't okay.

It was hard to trust a God who allowed those things to happen in the first place.

Until one day, wrapped in the remote forest of western North Carolina, God touched my deep hurts and insecurities in a very personal way.

Matt stood beside me in the church we were visiting with friends. As he shifted his weight to the back of his feet, his arm brushed against my leg, startling me. Distracted, I'd forgotten he was there. Slowly, I opened my eyes while rhythmic voices and lifted hands reunited me with the worship service in progress.

I traced my mental absence. As praise and worship began, I had lifted my voice in song with the rest. Yet, somewhere along the way I discovered myself, eyes closed, with an overwhelming longing for God's presence. To experience him. Hear him. To see him somehow.

Satan taunted me. "Who do you think you are—Moses? You can't *see* God."

Oh, but I can.

I leaned in. "Lord, I need to see you in my life. What do *you* desire for me? What are your plans, your future for me? And, will I *ever* escape these lingering hurts?"

Within minutes I felt an uneasiness in my heart, a restless pull that brought to mind each person, plan, or agenda I had placed above my desire to experience (see) God. Relationships. Career. Fears and insecurities.

When will you fully release each of these situations to me? The question pressed my mind.

God was done with my lip service; he meant a total surrender. I'd been at this crossroads before. I'd tried to scoot through with minimal compliance, but this time I knew God required *complete* surrender.

I mentally recounted each person and each situation by name. As some really tough memories passed through, I remained focused on God—his attributes and character battling for a front-of-mind spot as he and I walked through the hard stuff. Together, we journeyed toward a trust that would ultimately reveal his heart. A heart that longs to capture those things used against us, to turn them into refreshing streams of renewal (for our benefit and the benefit of others).

If we trust him, if we surrender to his work in our lives, he promises that we will grow stronger, that we will experience him like never before, and that we will be able to connect others to the truth that lies only in him.[49]

God is all-powerful and all-knowing.
He is good, merciful, gracious, and sovereign.
And if he has a plan, I want in on it.

By the time God and I finished processing, I could truly say I wanted to "see" him in my life more than I wanted to control what happened anymore. If there was a purpose, I was ready to accept it and move into it.

A sweet warmth filled me like a sip of spiced apple cider on a cool autumn morning.

I see you now, Lord. I see the times I've manipulated circumstances against your will. I see the many places I've robbed you. I see the life experiences available for your use. Help me to trust, Lord, that you do have good things that can come from this.

It was here that Matt bumped into me, and I rejoined what was going on around me. Normally less demonstrative in my worship, I joyfully lifted my hands heavenward, sharing in audible praises to a God who delights in revealing himself. How do we surrender? We trust enough to hand him the controls. He has them already, but oh how it warms his heart when we make this intentional sacrifice.

Each surrender–opportunity we encounter offers a costly choice, yet holds a precious gift.

While I don't know the meaning behind your suffering, what you've been through, I do know there's a beautiful gift any sufferer receives: empathy. Just ask Paul. In a deeply personal letter to the church, Paul shares his heart for these hurts of life, how through the pain we can learn to comfort others.[50]

> He gives you something you can then give away, which grows into full-formed lives . . . so that you can be generous in every way, producing with us great praise to God.[51]

Can we find meaning in this, these painful hurts of life? Without debating theology, I'll say this: when we meet other hurting women who are facing similar circumstances, we know the depth of that pain, so we can respond with a unique and very personal compassion. And God can use that in big ways.

Seeking God

Father,

While you are much more deserving of praise than hounding questions, I'm afraid the pain of what's happened to me often blocks me from completely surrendering to you.

There's this raging internal battle between a heart that longs to understand, that craves your loving comfort, and a scorned woman who would much rather blame. Why would you allow such things to happen, Lord? Why didn't you protect me? Where were you? Why did this happen?

Help me focus on your truth—it's the only thing that will lead me into complete healing and wholeness. I need your grace—lots of grace—to get me to the place where I can surrender to your sovereign hand. Please strengthen my trust in you, help me to hold high my little white flag. Reward me with the liberty that comes from real surrender.

That you would want my pain, my brokenness, my ashes, in exchange for your grace and mercy? You love me that much? Help me to accept this love, this beauty as you restore the places long devastated.

With arms uplifted, I praise you for the restoring work you are doing in my heart.

Amen.

THE VOICE STUDIO:

Responding to God's Call to Develop Our Voices

Facing That Thing We Wish to Hide

1. Do you struggle with God's sovereignty? Do you believe he is in control? That he has a plan? Why?

2. What does the idea of complete surrender to God do to you? Are you ready to surrender the need to know why?

3. Have you ever struggled with God's decisions?

4. Is there a loss you have failed to grieve? What is it, and what are some ways you could honor that loss now?

5. Mark Buchanan says, "What *will* happen matters more than what *has* happened." Do you agree? Why?

6. In what ways do you battle negativity? How could you reverse that thinking?

7. If you took one of life's most painful events and deleted it—wiped it from ever happening—is there anything (outside of the actual event, perhaps something that happened because of the event) that you could regret losing?

8. How can we "trust God to use the best and worst of our lives for his purposes"? What would that look like?
9. How do you imagine others perceive you?
10. What's next? If you could see into your future beyond any lingering pain, what do you think God might have in in store?

What's on Your Mind

Taming Unhealthy Emotions

Happy is the [wo]man who has broken the chains which hurt the mind . . .
~Ovid

A crisp September wind slides into my first open-windowed day of the year. I love fresh air, but the summer's scathing heat has not allowed the throwing back of curtains, the raising of windows.

It's the eleventh day of the month—a tender day for most as their own fire-locked memory holds fresh to the mind a senseless pain, a fear evoked by evil. My own scars cut fresh, even now. While I'm not a direct victim of 9/11—my fallout far removed from any terrorist attack—I too had been robbed of a sense of security. But long before that day.

My immediate reaction to the events of September 11, 2001, was passive and self-consumed. I had long ago crumbled under an emotional pain that numbed me, leaving me completely unresponsive. Rather than an immediate concern for our country and lost lives, those horrifying explosions simply echoed the pain of my own internal nightmare.

An inner rawness (a barbaric unfeelingness)
can tempt an unhealed heart,
callousing our compassion until it turns cold.

I stood, feet planted in front of the television, unable to accept, unable to process. Not because of what had happened to our country, but rather what had happened to me years before, and what *was* happening in my own home office just five minutes before that national attack.

An argument with my then-husband had turned violent. His hand clutched my long, red hair and whipped my head into my desk chair just as the phone rang. On the fall to the floor, I grabbed the receiver. The call was from my ex-husband, a veteran, a good man with whom I shared a daughter, a man who held an ongoing concern for me.

"Jo Ann," his voice was weak. "Turn on your television." He knew I never watched it.

"It's really not a good time—"

"Turn on the TV, Jo Ann. And check on Tabitha," he said, his voice growing louder. "Call back if you need me."

I hung up the phone and made my way to the television.

"What are you doing?" My husband roared. "That's like you to walk away. You know, we wouldn't be having these problems if you had torn up those divorce papers like I told you. You're ruining our marriage by keeping them."

I rubbed the side of my head. *I surely have my part in some of these arguments; antagonizing an angry man is never a good marriage-builder. But those papers were not the problem—they were the answer.*

Along with millions of others, I turned on the television in time to watch the second plane slice the South Tower of the World Trade Center. Fire and smoke raged incomprehensible. Pandemonium overtook the streets, the city, the country.

My husband joined me in the family room. He panicked, insisted the world was coming to an end. *How many others must have thought the same.*

My world had long been over. I stood frozen. Shell-empty, soul-depleted. *Outside of my control, outside of my concern.*

I watched myself dial the number of Tabitha's middle school. "We're aware of the situation, and the children are safe," the teacher said.

I believed her.

After I ended the call, my husband's predictable remorse kicked in (earlier than normal this time due to the national crisis) but his rote apology fell flat just the same.

Once more, the phone rang. It was my morning business appointment calling to cancel.

"But we're a good 700 miles from the situation, and safe," I assured him. "Why wouldn't we still discuss our potential partnership—we don't really want to push this back do we, just because of *this*?"

Swimming on the surface is easy
when you're steeped in denial.

I imagine my insolence shocked him because he relented.

It was easy for me to pursue my day as normal. *Messed up, yes, I now know.* Something so catastrophic and world-changing and I couldn't even feel it, couldn't begin to comprehend the pain of thousands of lives for my own raging misery.

Should you be tempted to judge me, consider that my brain had been hijacked, healthy communication and comprehension blocked. Depression does that sort of thing, alters the brain's biology, changes the heart's beat. My outward actions had simply followed my mind into a cave, dark and deep.

Sometimes a searing heat can make you see,
better ground you to reality.

Those Times We Fall into Thinking-Traps

Ever found yourself trapped in a cave? The times in life when negative thought-motivated behaviors run so deep you simply can't find your way out.

Elijah, a bold and robust mountain man who walked intimately with the Lord, understands. He too had a serious problem with negative thoughts, the backlash of emotional abuse, threats, and manipulation skewing his perspective. (Faulty thinking can do that to a person unaware.)

In 1 Kings 18, we find the normally forceful prophet, Elijah, insidiously depressed. He should have been celebrating a great victory, having just killed all the false prophets of Baal at Mount Carmel. Unfortunately, Elijah's success didn't sit well with Queen Jezebel, a woman who had puppeted an entire nation, including her husband, King Ahab, for years.

But Elijah, in this one eventful afternoon, had unexpectedly clipped her control. Enraged, Jezebel threatened to take Elijah's life—and he believed her.

Elijah had just returned from a literal mountaintop experience, where God completely annihilated the enemy. Hundreds of men wiped out, on Elijah's watch. And now? Now he's running scared of a woman. One woman.

After a solid day of running through the desert, he settled beneath a lone juniper tree. Here, underneath the pole-like stems, Elijah gave in to the negative thoughts hammering his mind. He begged God to end everything. "Enough of this, GOD. Take my life."[52]

This from the man God hand-picked to turn around the spiritual decline of Israel? A man so close to God that he was credited with bringing the dead back to life and raining fire from heaven? The once-mighty prophet now sat crumpled and depressed beneath a tree. Angry. Bitter. Isolated.

There's such a danger in drifting,
the gradual slipping away from truth.

I guess we women aren't the only ones vulnerable to lies. Elijah had fallen for one, too. At a time when he could have been used to make a difference, he fled. With two differing beliefs warring within him, it was easier to believe the lies. Rather than focus on (and rest in) all the powerful, supernatural moments he had experienced with God, Elijah chose to believe that an idol-worshiping, prophet-killing queen was bigger than the God he had long served and loved.

Elijah had walked under God's miracle-performing power and provision, yet he feared for his life, doubting that God could or would protect him *this time*. He gave in to Jezebel's threats, all the while knowing God had the power to save him. God had proven faithful, but Elijah's deep-seated insecurities felt bigger than God.

Elijah started to believe his own lie, accept it as truth. Isn't that the natural bent of a wounded heart? Hear something long enough and we start to believe it.

I've always wondered something, though: If Jezebel got a messenger close enough to Elijah with a life-threat, why didn't she have him taken out then? Seems to me Jezebel's threat was a conscious, intelligent attempt to control, to manipulate.

Manipulators can derail God's purpose for your life if you let them.

When Self-Pity Drives Us to the Hills

Many of us are blinded by fear despite God's promises. We're angry. We isolate. We may even beg to die.

Exhausted from the tasks of leadership, Moses did it: "I can't do this by myself. It's too much. . . . Do me a favor and kill me. I've seen enough, had enough."[53]

Furious that God saved his enemies, Jonah did it: "Kill *me*! I'm better off dead."[54]

Overwrought with discouragement that no one listened to his warnings from God, Jeremiah did it: "I'm worn out; I can't do it any longer. . . . Why did I ever leave [that] womb? Life's been nothing but trouble and tears."[55]

I've done it, too. How about you? Maybe you've not begged to die, but have you ever felt like giving up? Ever fallen for dangerous lies, even while you knew the truth?

Doublethink. That's what George Orwell (in the novel *1984*) calls this, and we do it far too often. And it messes with us.

> Doublethink means the power of holding two contradictory beliefs in one's mind simultaneously, and accepting both of them . . . to hold simultaneously two opinions which cancelled out, knowing them to be contradictory and believing in both of them.[56]

What are we doing here—in this land of doublethink, this land of contradiction and confusion?

It's the same question God asked of Elijah. Even after God helped him recover from suicidal thoughts, Elijah ran another forty days only to tuck himself away in a cave.

But God continued the pursuit. "Why are you here?" he asked.

Steeped in denial. Elijah decides to play the blame game. (We never really get very far from the influence of Adam and Eve, do we?) With forty days' worth of practiced excuses, he presented a pretty good argument.

"I've done my best, God. People have lied to me and against me, and now they are trying to kill me." Elijah said.

What he didn't say, and should have said, was, "I'm scared. A faint-hearted coward." And even though God knew that to be true, he still listened to Elijah, fully listened, honoring every hurting word (1 Kings 19).

"I am here." God acknowledged Elijah's pain with his very presence. *I'm here, Elijah—I've got this.*

We aren't alone in the cave;
the bending of light cannot stop the presence of God.
In the darkness, God offers a new focus:
He is with us.

Have you ever been so deeply immersed in a disagreement, pointing fingers, defending yourself, that you keep arguing unnecessarily? That's sort of what Elijah did. "I've done my best, the people have lied, and they are trying to kill me," Elijah repeated his earlier complaint.

Can't you just see God shaking his head? *Why does he not get that I can handle this? If only he would face the truth.*

Without judgment or blame, dripping with grace, God tried once again. This time, he challenged Elijah to stretch his eyes beyond his current circumstances, offering him a fresh perspective. God's assignment for Elijah? Go back and anoint others. Purely my speculation here, but I suspect a fresh blessing is birthed in the pits of pain. That's just the sort of thing God can do in a cave.

There's an undeniable healing power
in telling the truth to someone who validates you
by simply listening—
honor washes away the stench of shame.

It's Time for Some On-Purpose Thinking

On September 11, 2001, I watched one of our nation's worst tragedies unfold, yet my anesthetized heart pumped indifference. My own war took precedence, leaving me numb and unnervingly detached from the pain of others.

A dangerous confusion leaks into our minds when the soul has been wounded, the heart split. I wish there was a magic wand to wave it all away—the pain and fallout. While we might not be able to change what's happened to us, we *can* change the aftermath, the future.

We are not trapped in these hurts of life.

I wasn't trapped, no matter how much it felt that way. The abuse I was facing (and had faced in different ways for years) may have explained my emotional distortions, but it couldn't excuse them. The way out for me was a strong support system that grounded me in the truth of God's Word and a willingness to speak up about my situation. That, and an accountability that prevented further abuse in my home (it really is okay to call for outside help sometimes, and at times that may mean a call to the police).

The person who tried (or tries) to hold us down, to silence us, is not the real enemy. The battle is in our minds—it is on this battlefield that our quality of life will be determined.

Being honest about our hidden hurts is important.
To heal the pain, you must acknowledge it.

Like a child, our brains pretty much do what we train them to do. The more we repeat something, the deeper it works into our belief systems. Somehow the act of repetition creates these easy-to-travel pathways in our brains that enable good thoughts to form good habits. However, the same works for bad thoughts; they form bad habits. Bad, purpose-robbing, life-draining habits.

These thoughts condition our beliefs. Over time we become trained to a particular environment—especially if changes occur gradually—and we accept them as normal or impossible to change. Sort of like the boiling frog story. You know—the metaphor where if you place a frog in boiling water, he'll jump out, but if you put him in cold water that's slowly heated then he doesn't perceive the danger until it's too late and he's cooked.

Frog or not, negative thought patterns can become habits, training our behaviors as they dominate and run our brains. Eventually we sink into these habits, and our brains get stuck in this antagonistic place, this boiling water that may eventually cook us.

Just like Elijah, the lies we tell ourselves can be as powerful as truth. *I'm damaged goods. I'm not pretty enough. Not good enough. I'm too fat. Too skinny. It's all my fault.*

Because we've heard things like this from authoritative and persuasive people, we've taken them in as truth. Years of this lead to automatic negative self-talk as we inwardly repeat these diminishing phrases. But we *can* change the way we think if we consistently and deliberately create links to calm and truthful emotions. We *can* refuse to allow these negative thoughts to dominate our behaviors. We have to retrain our brain's natural default, line it up with God's way of thinking.

Position God as the Gate-Keeper of your thoughts.
Ask him to condition your brain to think positively.
To capture lies. To hope. To change.

While we can't always control the thoughts that land in our minds, we can decide whether to own them or not. And we have about three seconds to make that decision. That's something Bill Irwin taught me early on, how to prevent unhealthy thoughts from hanging around. He called it the "three-second rule." He challenged me to corral any negative thoughts that hit my brain within three seconds. To identify and deal with them immediately.

I get this. I know what it's like to be held captive mentally, to hold back in shame, to live in fear of rejection, ridicule, or embarrassment. There are those days still when my doublethinking runs rampant—the hard days when the rip tide of insecurity wins. But growing are the days I manage to allow truth to override my emotions. The Selah-moments when I return to the truth of God's Word as an accurate guide for right-thinking.

The days where I barter my irrational feelings for God's grace and mercy—those are my freedom-laced days, my celebrated days of independence. Those are the times I stand stronger, more confident in this Jesus-walk.

It's a whole new way of living; a makeover of sorts.

I love the DIY (do-it-yourself) trend that consumes the country these days. The mere fact that millions of women are willing to jump in, hands and feet, heart and soul, and commit to the completion of some unique project captivates me.

I wonder if you're willing to join me for a makeover—only instead of DIY, we'll call it DIG (do-it-with-God). Yes, ladies, it's time to get the kind of makeover that will transform our lives. Some of us may be redoing only one room, while others of us are going for the whole house. (You won't catch me judging, I'm signed up for the complete redo.)

Much like a library, our brains hold an archive of attitudes, beliefs, and expectations, but the records are based on *all we've ever done.* Everything we've ever thought, seen, or heard rests within these walls—some truthful, some not. The health of our emotions hangs in the balance of this personal brain library, hinging on whether we can focus on the truth messages. And that's where we're going next. For this remodel to take shape, we must examine our belief system, rebuild it on a more secure foundation.

Will we allow God's thoughts to redesign ours?

Much like learning any new skill, this will require practice.

I remember when I taught my daughter, Tabitha, to drive. I was a single mother at the time and we had only one car. A stick shift. Not only did Tabitha have to learn to drive, she had to learn to maneuver a manual transmission at the same time. A dying art, I know.

I confess I wasn't the best teacher; I probably shouldn't have closed my eyes so much. But through the grinding of many gears, Tabitha repeatedly practiced the clutch release point. After countless tears and untold threats to quit, she finally discovered the exact point where the clutch engages and how to combine that with the shifter. Working the clutch and shifting the gears soon became second nature to her, but neither she nor I will ever forget those times of practice.

It was hard. We both got frustrated, wondering if she could really do it. But she wouldn't quit. I suspect her motivation was that she wasn't allowed to date until she was capable of driving any type of car on her own. Regardless, Tabitha soon celebrated her freedom of driving, and I rested in knowing she was prepared for the road ahead with skills that would lead her to a safe place, if ever she needed.

Why It All Starts with an Intentional Choice

God's truth will radically alter our perspective, if we allow. My friend Aj understands. From a young age, her mind and heart had been skillfully tilled for manipulation by authority figures. She grew up a people pleaser—one with a real problem establishing healthy boundaries and standing for what she believed was true.

In a former marriage, Aj's husband had taken an extreme interest in the internet and was spending hours online behind locked doors. Aj suspected a pornography addiction, but uncovered a dark relationship even she hadn't imagined.

Aj's husband had built a relationship with a local pastor, one he'd found online. Her husband and the pastor talked for hours on the phone as if they were long-lost friends with much catching up to do.

Not long afterward, Aj's husband invited the pastor and his family for Thanksgiving dinner.

"That actually sounded fun," Aj said. "I loved to cook, and Thanksgiving dinner is a favorite of mine to make. I was a little nervous about our new guest but soon became so preoccupied with preparing an enjoyable meal that the anxiety faded."

After putting the last touches on the elaborate turkey dinner, the pastor, his wife, and their small child arrived. With a warm welcome, Aj offered appetizers, drinks, and a *Veggie Tales* DVD for the little one to watch. The pastor quickly declined the suggestion for a movie, and Aj's party moved into a lovely meal packed with delicious food and surface conversation.

After dinner, Aj once again offered entertainment for the child. "Why don't I slide in this DVD, so the adults can talk?"

An uncomfortable silence fell in the room as everyone turned toward Aj with a frown, including her husband. The pastor spoke first, "Sorry. We don't watch television. Television is a gateway to hell and it's not how I raise my family or run my church. We are expected to be holy at all times, and that is not holy."

So much for surface conversation.

The pastor and Aj's husband then teamed up to deliver a belief system that jolted her beyond comprehension.

"After laying out the criteria for inclusion in their church, they wanted to debate theology. I was up for it. I read my Bible and was willing to discuss it," Aj said. "But as they continued, it felt like everything

I'd learned about the Bible was going to have to be unlearned to attend their church."

The pastor's next words were much more than a petty distinction. "There is no such thing as the Trinity."

The smell of turkey and sweet potatoes lingered. The dishes were piled to the ceiling and Aj's feet were tired. Her hostess gene wanted to offer the freshly brewed coffee with pie and beg for peace, but instead, she sat in her chair chained to the dinner table in a shocking battle for truth.

"What do you mean there is no such thing as the Trinity?" Aj asked. "What about the book of Genesis where it says, 'Let us make man in Our image,' or what about Jesus praying in the garden—who was he talking to? Was he schizophrenic?"

The pastor replied, "I am not familiar with that passage."

Until this time, the conversation was fairly civil, but the more Aj pressed for truth the stronger the pastor's tone grew, until he ultimately leaned over Aj and demanded, "You have to deny the Trinity." Her husband nodded in agreement.

With a focus on the quiet submission of wives to their husbands, the pastor and husband team stood shoulder-to-shoulder, towering over Aj, citing biblical doctrine.

Head down and shoulders slumped, she shook her head in disbelief. *This is absurd. Stupid.* Aj sought the eyes of the pastor's wife for support, relief, some semblance of truth, but was met with disdain.

"You must deny the Trinity exists," the two continued.

"After nearly two hours, I collapsed in my chair, unable to go on," Aj said. "Fine, the way you describe it I don't believe in the Trinity . . ." Exhausted from the confrontation, she excused herself, escaping to the silence and safety of her dark bedroom.

A flower dies easily when it's already wilting.

"How could someone take something so tender and precious, my relationship with God, and take advantage of it?" Aj wondered.

With an all-consuming sadness, she crawled into her bed fully dressed. *Why did you leave me alone to face that, God?* She curled under the covers into a fetal position, eventually crying herself to sleep.

Aj woke to an answer pressing her spirit. "The next time someone asks you to deny the Trinity, tell them no. You know the truth." The stern but loving words from God blanketed her heart.

"Oh God, forgive me. How I've been deceived, and broken your heart in the process. Can you fix this? Can you bring me back to truth, to you?" Aj said.

Finally falling into a peaceful sleep, Aj woke the next morning with an intense desire to cling to God's truth—no matter what. She was forced to take responsibility to direct her mind, regardless of heartbreaking, nerve-racking circumstances that eventually wrecked her marriage.

The Things We (Should) Tell Ourselves

Like Aj, I'm learning the importance of allowing God and his Word to direct my mind, to dictate my behavior. We simply can't rely on emotions to guide us; we must let God show us how to feel. Through his Word, God untwists the lies that tempt us to act on false feelings.

My now-husband, Matt, is a comedian and sleight-of-hand magician who travels across the country. He is a renowned entertainer who uses his talent to both entertain and draw people into a closer relationship with God. At times, I travel with him as he ventures into various towns with his uplifting humor that masks the deeper call of discipleship.

A while back, I tagged along with Matt to North Carolina for an event. That evening, he touched on a subject I'm passionate about: self-talk. The concept is nothing new. We all do it. But these things we silently tell ourselves—they matter.

Are we telling ourselves the truth?

Research shows much of our *internal* dialogue is negative messages rooted in low self-worth. The kind of talk that spoils a soul, wears down a spirit. We must change this; we must fight for positivity in spite of our outward circumstances.

Are we encouraging ourselves, strengthening ourselves? Or, are we constantly judging ourselves? Worrying what others think? Paralyzed when someone attacks our character? Afraid if someone uncovers the real person inside, they won't like us? Pretending to be strong while everything inside cries weak, defeated?

A couple minutes into his talk, Matt garnered my full attention. "We need to tell our emotions how to feel, deliberately deciding to apply the Word. To meditate on it day and night."

Tell our emotions how to feel? First I can choose to think differently, and now I can tell my emotions how to feel? My mind whirled at the possibility of no longer being controlled by the opinions of others or my own insecurities. From my chair in a quiet corner in the back of the church, I sat up straight, grabbed my iPhone, and went to my notes app, readying myself. *Alright, how do I do this?*

Meditate on God's Word day and night. It sounds mystical, doesn't it? Unattainable. But this meditation Matt spoke of is not just a thought, but an actual sound—spoken words. As with the English language, Hebrew words can be translated differently within various contexts, but we often see *meditate* referred to as an audible mental reflection of biblical truth.

As you've seen, I love digging into the deeper meanings of words. And my close companion, *Strong's Concordance*, shows me here how God actually commands us to never stop speaking the truth of his Word (Josh. 1:8, Prov. 8:7). How he encourages us to repeat (all day long if we must) his plans, his truth—when people hate us for no reason, when we are patronized, mocked, hurt, lied to, and blamed for everything (Ps. 35:28). And ultimately, how we are to tell others of his healing and goodness (Ps. 71:24).

In all those verses, the word *meditate* has a root meaning of murmuring, muttering, or even growling, all of which indicate a spoken word of some type. Just think—all that murmuring and growling we've been doing is a *natural* tendency; we've just chosen the wrong words to focus on.

> My Word is not void of power.
>
> My people are void of speech. . . . By observing circumstances they have lost sight of My Word. They even speak that which the enemy says, and they destroy their own inheritance by corrupt communication of fear and unbelief.[57]

Matt was right: we need to tell ourselves how to feel. Out loud. Loud-enough-to-drown-out-deception-and-discouragement out loud.

"Self, I'm going to tell you what God says about you," Matt continued in his talk. "God has already said I am an overcomer. He loves me and I am worthy, valued. And what I have to say matters."

Every day, we have a choice about how we feel.
What does today hold for you?
Peace and joy? Or angst and strife?

This Is Hard Stuff When You Don't Know How to Trust

Remember Elizabeth (from Chapter Two) who found a false sense of community nestled within the lure of gangs? After years of sexual abuse, addictions, and abusive relationships, she believed she was far beyond the reach of Jesus.

> *I had recently graduated college and was headed into the Christian music industry. I had recorded in Nashville, and when I wasn't touring the country, I spent most of my days teaching purity and abstinence.*
>
> *I returned to my parents after a weekend youth conference. My mom sat next to me on the couch, reciting notes she had taken while I was away. As the author of the curriculum, Mom had suggestions to improve the content.*

"How about this?" She asked, pointing to a particular edit.

"No, I can't do that, Mom." I said.

"Alright, if you look at this spot you could see how if you—"

"Mom, really, I can't make any changes."

"What, Elizabeth, are you pregnant or something?" She laughed, never imagining the possibility.

I hung my head. Surely this is the last straw. *I was the oldest daughter of a pastor, teaching purity and abstinence, pregnant and unmarried—a mere month after an extended stay in the hospital due to an eating disorder.*

My parents had seen me through much rebellion; six years earlier had allowed me to come home after my first year of college when I was brutally raped and pregnant (although I lost that baby). I was certain they would throw me out this time.

I'm so stupid—pretty sure this was not the dream my parents had for me. I'm worthless. Messed up. How could they possibly love me?

My parents remained calm and rational. I wasn't prepared for that. I messed up. Yell at me. Tell me how dumb that was and that I've gone way too far this time.

I had decisions to make, and they weren't easy ones. I went back and forth about whether to keep the child myself or give him up for adoption—and admittedly, thoughts of terminating the pregnancy made their way in there a few times.

A baby changes everything.

As a young, single parent, I certainly had my struggles raising my son. I walked a few more years of disbelief. How could anyone ever love someone like me—especially God? *But I soon encountered Jesus. At an event no one thought I would even attend, I finally grasped the love of the Father.*

Psalm 139:14 permeated my being, "I am fearfully and wonderfully made." I was a princess of the King. What little girl doesn't want to be a princess? *I posted this verse on my bathroom mirror, in my car, at my desk at work. I carried it in my pocket and tucked inside my Bible.*

This was a startling revelation to a young woman who didn't trust, didn't love. I understood God to be a wrathful God—learned that in my years of Christian education—but this God who loved me was new to me.

Alongside a Christian counselor, God soon opened up the truth of his Word in a startling way. I had long known about sin and messing up, but I never heard the rest of the story: God was a God of love, concern, mercy, and grace. Oh, I pushed back with my deceptive half-truth understandings, but my counselor asked me to dig deeper, to seek and digest the full truth.

Time in the book of Isaiah softened my view of this vengeful God who was out to get me. I spent my entire life running from his wrath when all he wanted me to do was surrender to his love.

Who has time for grace and love
when you're simply trying to survive?

As I moved to genuine surrender I understood God hadn't let me down. Yes, people let me down, but God somehow used it for good. He was with me, even when I didn't think so. He protected me in ways I'm unaware of, having completely spared my life at times. God was and always will be my Protector. He does love me; he rescued me and set me free. That's the sort of thing that happens when you dare to fully believe God.

When the Truth Carries You Forward

"What's the worst that can really happen?" My friend and life coach Holley asked me.

I was having a hard time moving away from negativity and fear. Holley was sensitive to the situation but wanted to corral my anxiety.

"I would fail." I said.

"And what would happen if you failed?" Holley pressed.

Like an oyster seeking its pearl,
we will have to be vulnerable,
but in the end we produce a rare gem,
a beauty otherwise unattainable.

That question and a few others made me realize the fear I felt wasn't as powerful as I had imagined. It was a helpful exercise because it made me realize that my fears probably wouldn't happen, and even if they did, it wouldn't be the catastrophe I imagined.

Sometimes we have to walk all the way through our negative thoughts, identifying them, then reframing them with truth *before* we can let them go.

Retraining our brains is not some overblown idea, my friend. It's life-changing truth. The kind of perpetual truth that heals a woman's heart, equips her to strip away fears, doubts, and insecurities—every single day. Yesterday's victory doesn't mean we don't challenge today's words.

Those words from others, these words we tell ourselves, they're often packed with lies. But lies unravel easily when lined up under Truth. It's not a passive thing, this choosing to trust God more than we trust our feelings. This is how we move into a healthy life: we use our voices to project God's truth into our futures. We speak more from God's power than from our hurts.

Can I pause here for a second? I just have to say that you look beautiful in these deep waters. God's stirring some genuine healing here, and you are making your way through the water with such grace and beauty. You inspire me.

In the beginning of our journey I imagine you dipped your toes in, tested the waters, but soon discovered the temperature was not so bad. You've been swimming strong for a while now. So, I think it's time for a break. A sneak preview of what's to come, we'll say.

You want to find your voice, to use your story to make a difference. And that's what God wants you to do. To borrow a concept from my mentor, Katie Brazelton, let's consider how some of your life experiences might possibly hint at God's future plans.

Grab your journal and write through these questions, giving them the time they deserve. You're worth it. I'll catch up with you again in the next chapter, where we're going to go deeper still.

- What do you consider important in life?
- What are your top values, the unwritten guidelines you live by (i.e., goals, appearance, health, reputation, Jesus . . .)?
- Does your lifestyle reflect what you consider most important?
- How do you plan to trust God's truth and use it to guide your emotions?
- What life experiences have you most enjoyed?

God's Healing Words

Precious Daughter,

I have made you just as you are. Since I don't make anything less than wonderful, please stop doubting yourself. Stop discounting my work. You are a person worthy of respect, a person set apart and distinct—my creation, fashioned to suit my purposes. Do not allow the hurtful words and actions of others to devalue what I have created.

As you focus on me for right-thinking, I will help you avoid the negative thinking traps. You will learn healthy ways of thinking that lead you into your purpose, lead you into me.

Remember, you have a choice about how to feel. Choose my peace and joy over the angst and strife that threatens. Tell your emotions how to feel, line them up with my Word. Meditate on my truths day and night so that my Words will drench your thoughts like water saturating dry ground, infiltrating the subsurface so you can be replenished as needed .

Abide with me, remain in close relationship with me so that I can always point you to truth, and to the full life I have planned for you.

Maintain a positive mind-set, this choice for healthy emotions and abundant living—no matter what. Diligently protect your mind, the place from which all things flow. Filter the words you say to yourself (and to others) that cheapen your divine worth.

Listen to me, once again: I will love you, direct you, and uphold your worth.[58] *Cling to this truth when your feelings tell you otherwise.*

Love,
The Creator of Perfection

THE VOICE STUDIO:

Responding to God's Call to Develop Our Voices

Breaking the Chains of Negative Thinking

1. In what ways have you felt trapped by your thoughts or emotions?
2. What lies have you believed in the past? What lies do you think you might be susceptible to even now? What do you do when you hear these lies? What could you do differently?
3. Are you a stuffer? How does this impact your relationships? Your life overall?
4. If it's possible to "train our brains," what could this mean for your future? What positive changes do you see happening?
5. What sort of things do you tell yourself? Do these things ever surprise you when you stop to think about the real message? Does this self-talk empower you, or hinder you?

6. How did Jesus confront negative thoughts? How should you?

7. How can you let God's truth impact your daily life? Guide what you think about?

8 Do you feel it is possible to honor God with a hurting heart—to live our lives in a way that others would see him in spite of what we're going through? Why or why not?

9. What are five of your core values—your deeply held beliefs, priorities, and principles—that guide your daily decisions? What is so important to you that you feel as if you can't live without it? Family? Success? Relationships?

10. How can you prepare your heart to hear God's truth? What are some ways you can meditate on his Word?

The Wellspring of Life

Cultivating a Healthy, Confident Heart

Now, with God's help, I shall become myself.
~Søren Kierkegaard

With her Bugs Bunny satchel, five-year-old Theresa Harvard Johnson ran down the sidewalk, skirting the swaths of broken concrete. The morning's kindergarten songs rang through her head like the tolling of bells after a wedding ceremony. As Theresa made her way home from school, the hidden wars of her household were far from her mind—until she turned the corner near her duplex in the middle of government family housing.

Theresa's satchel fell to the ground as her eyes landed on her half-naked mother rolling in the dirt in her front yard. An elderly neighbor grabbed Theresa, squeezing her hand. "She's having a nervous breakdown, baby," she said. "Just stay here with me."

"Take me away," Theresa's mother screamed to the paramedics. "I don't want my baby to see me like this."

Theresa watched helplessly as the medical technicians strapped her mother to a gurney, loading her into the back of the ambulance, then pulling away.

"Daddy had to take her to the doctor again," Theresa's father told her later.

"Why Daddy? Why can't Mama be home with us?"

When she did come home, Mama spent many days squatted in the corner, rocking and crying. The poison of her mother's schizophrenia seeded young Theresa's life. Early on, she witnessed the abuse of her brother and sisters, a deep-rooted fear and rage consuming her.

Years passed and her mother's mental illness finally peaked.

"Whores belong on the street. Don't come back here—he's my husband!" Mama's words reverberated behind thirteen-year-old Theresa as she wiped the blood from her lips; her mother's punch still burning.

A barefooted Theresa stumbled onto the street wearing only a t-shirt and slip. She spent countless nights dozing in abandoned cars and walking dark city streets to avoid the pain at home, until a concerned neighbor reported the situation and Theresa entered the foster care system. The darkness of suicidal thoughts decorated Theresa's teen years; the searing relief of self-injury her only distraction.

Am I invisible here? I am nothing but a big mistake. I can't possibly matter to anyone. No one even sees me, or wants me. I hate myself. I wish I could die.

On impulse, one last effort to matter, Theresa confronted her fear and reached out to tell others the things that hurt. But the devastating response merely raised the temperature on an already blistered heart.

"This man had sex with me—and he hurt me," Theresa said to an adult she trusted.

"Don't make a big deal out of it, okay? Just let it go."

Let it go? Okay, if it doesn't matter to them, it must not matter. I knew I didn't matter to anyone, nothing but trash.

How does one deal with such demented unreliability? When it feels like no one cares, when we can't believe in ourselves, we tend to avoid challenges. *Is it even worth the fight?* We drown out the one true voice that begs for a chance, because we are afraid. We drown it out with noise and distractions, anything to take away the pain—yet we remain afraid. Afraid to speak, afraid not to; afraid of losing ourselves, afraid of finding ourselves.

Theresa carried a flourishing insecurity into her adult life where she married, had children, and built an exciting career couched in respect and recognition, along with a good paycheck. But her masked life eventually crumbled.

"I fought so hard to just get over it, but this brewing dislike of myself boiled into hatred. My marriage was a wreck. I was totally detached, consumed with a volatile anger. My children were afraid of me; I spent 90 percent of my time enraged and the remaining 10 percent in tears. The storms in my head were only quieted by a medication that left me in a fog."

If we aren't okay,
how can we expect the people around us be okay?
Shame, guilt, self-loathing, and insecurity,
they seep into how we relate, how we parent,
how we work, how we live.

"I was petrified I would be discovered," Theresa said. "What would people think when they realized my life was all a lie. A deep darkness overtook me, hopelessness consuming me. Those death wishes from my childhood—they returned. *I'd be better off dead. Everyone around me would be better off without me.* I drove at high speeds, stopping mere inches from ending my life. I counted pills over and over as I vacillated between life and death. I was institutionalized, medicated, discarded—so out of it that I didn't want to live. And this was as a Christian.

"So many bad things had happened I couldn't remember the good. Good times were scattered in there but when your mind is messed up, sometimes all you see is pain. The lack of nurturing affirmation and love over the years nearly killed me. I was dying of depression, dying from a lack of love, acceptance, and belonging. Death taunted me as the only escape."

When There's Nothing Left to Do but Walk Through

In spite of imminent danger, David boldly and calmly walked through the darkest of valleys—confidently knowing the journey's end. Psalm 23 recounts another familiar story, but the trail of these well-known words models an uncommon courage that helps us think more clearly in the face of confusion and fear.

David had a secret: in spite of how things appeared, he relentlessly held to the truth of God's character. And he was openly rewarded for his courage. David was not just safe and delivered from danger, but also honored and treated like the royalty God destined him to be. Remember, this is the same kid-shepherd whose own family held him in such low regard that his father didn't deem him worthy of including when told to bring all of his sons before Samuel for a ceremonial feast.[59]

How do we gain this simple, unclouded confidence as we walk through the dark places? This nerve, this boldness to face what seems hard and terrifying? Much like the sheep that David was entrusted with, we hang close to the Shepherd. In Eastern culture the shepherd went in front of his flock to ensure safety, the sheep following behind—it was much easier to protect and lead them that way.

> *When God stands front and center,*
> *everything must go through him—*
> *even the wild and crazy that wants to take us out.*

There is a beautiful life-transforming power in the Shepherd presence of God. A shepherd used a simple rod and staff for authority and protection, deliverance and comfort. A rod—a common tool grasped by the shepherd's hand—guarded the sheep from falling into pits. And for those times they simply couldn't avoid the pits? That same tool was used to pull them out.

The rod was also used to inspect the sheep. Thick wool can hide a lot—sickness, disease, or wounds. Good shepherds routinely examined their sheep to uncover anything hidden. They pushed back the wool to check out the skin beneath, to see inside.

But the shepherd's staff? That offered a consolation and support otherwise unavailable. Used to draw the sheep, the gentle pressure of the staff against the sheep's side guided the animal out of harm's way.

Sometimes we don't realize the danger in straying.

These dark valleys, these shadows of death, we've seen our share. And in this search for our voices, we've tread some tough pathways. As we continue this journey to freedom, I can't promise you there won't be any hidden pits, that we won't be tempted back into traps of wrong thinking. We sheep can be pretty vulnerable in our stubbornness. Left to ourselves, we often stray from our Master's lead.

But I can promise you, if while we're on the path we do fall into the pit, the Shepherd's hand is there. Ahead of us. Out in front of us, ready to guide.

There are times all we can do is hold onto the Staff
—and believe.

With death taunting her, Theresa found herself in one horrible, miserable pit. But as promised, the Shepherd's hand was waiting.

As a board member for a local nonprofit, one evening she attended a banquet. A pastor who worked alongside her on the board reached out—not an easy task. In Theresa's mind, pastors were akin to used car salesmen and pimps. Over the years, their scare-her-to-salvation tactics had worn thin.

"Hi." The pastor extended his hand. "It's a shame we've served together on this board this long and don't know each other any better."

After a few minutes of idle conversation, the pastor said, "Jesus loves you, you know. He can heal your hurting heart."

At a time when hope threatens to never rise again,
the power in the simple truth of God's Word
can call one's spirit to attention, can transform a life.

What the pastor couldn't have known was that this night was meant to be Theresa's last. She had planned everything out. But there was something about this simple truth the pastor shared that she couldn't ignore. For once, Theresa believed the words of a pastor. Every. Single. Word.

This is my last opportunity for change. Theresa chose not to end her life that night.

But there were still hard choices to be made. *Would I choose my destiny, which is rooted in Jesus' plan for my life, or would I continue to live like I had for the past thirty-eight years?*

"Jesus, I need you to move and operate in my life. I need your presence, your understanding. I need you to speak to me. To heal me. I need to see you evident in my family," Theresa said. "I'll do anything."

And she meant it. Theresa saturated herself with God's voice, his words, and sound counsel until she learned to follow his presence, until she found her own voice. Today, she is a trained ministry leader who facilitates healing to other broken women.

Those dark-as-death valleys?
We no longer have to fear them.

Those Times Healing Comes with a Price Tag

"Do you want to get well?" Jesus once asked a sick man lying by a pool in Jerusalem.[60]

The Pool of Bethesda was known for healing people; common belief was that its swirls healed the first one in. Each day, hundreds of sick folks cluttered the five porches around the pool, hoping to be the one. But Jesus singled one lone man, asking him a barefaced question.

Like Theresa, the man had been sick for over thirty-eight years. It was all he knew—his days spent hanging out with other broken, dysfunctional people, assuming this was his place in the world. Always seeking, but never finding, complete wholeness.

Jesus countered with a new perspective, "Do you *want* to get well?"

I imagine the man's mental rehearsal. "Of course I do. But no one understands. There's no one to help me. I've tried everything I know. And worse, no one even cares."

Full of self-pity, focused solely on the injustice of it all, the invalid offered all the right excuses. *I've taken the right steps. I've prayed. Showed up when I didn't feel like it. Waited for other able-bodied people to help me. What else could I possibly do?*

I see a lot of me, a lot of you, in some of those excuses.

Jesus didn't judge. He didn't discount the man's suffering, or even address his lack of hope. He simply offered a cure, dependent on an intentional choice. "If you want to be well, I am available."

Most of us stay suspended somewhere between the pain of our circumstances and those right choices that lead to freedom, but there's always a day that can turn our lives around, if we watch for it and act on it. In spite of nearly four decades of wrong-thinking, the invalid decided to take Jesus at his word. Regardless of his emotions or the many failed attempts he'd walked through, the sick man refocused on Jesus and what Jesus believed for him.

> *Those times we can't believe in ourselves,*
> *those are the times we have to hold onto*
> *what others believe for us.*

God honored the choice, dictated a new future for him. "Take up your mat and walk."

Jesus poses the same question to us. "Do *you* want to get well?"

Before we launch into our own internal rant, let's consider the challenge: *Do we really want to be healed?* Because being healed changes everything.

The question indicates a choice—a necessary decision. If God shows us our role in the healing process, do we want it badly enough to accept? To "take up our mats and walk"? Are we fully willing to take on the responsibility of a purpose-filled life?

Sometimes it's easier to hide behind the familiar pain.
To replay the same old movie.
Repeat the same mistakes, blame the same people.
But that's not God's plan.

In our time together, we're learning how to stop listening to false voices, and how to recognize God's voice. We're breaking through old habits and negative patterns. Learning to think positively. So, how do we now honor this emerging person, this always-been-there-but-never-been-respected voice?

It's time to dive deeper. And the mama in me is coming out again—I want you to be prepared in advance. To know that the pressure can increase with depth.

But it's a manageable pressure, I promise. And the discovery of the beauty deep inside is worth it. Just keep looking up, and keep your mask clear—you'll do just great.

In Which We Get Armed for Life

Back when I was seventeen years old and had nowhere else to go, I joined the army. And I suffered a pretty rude awakening during boot camp—you would not believe how early those people expect you to get up, and the things they want you to do. I still have flashbacks about the things I chewed up, climbed over, and crawled through.

But the one thing I learned was how to fight. Girlie-girl me learned how to disassemble, clean, reassemble and shoot an M16. I even earned a sharpshooter badge.

Back then, it was unheard of for women to go to the front lines; we were molded into more of a support role. Yet they still trained us to fight. And while the training surely wasn't easy or fun, I understood its purpose. I can't say I appreciated it at the time, and I probably won't ever recognize its true value unless someday I land in a war zone.

During training, it was crucial for me to learn how to take apart my rifle; if I ever got caught in the middle of a fight and my weapon misfired or jammed, I would need to know what to do. God wants the same for us now. He wants to strengthen us, to train our hands for battle.[61]

God trains us to "fight fair and well,"
but he expects us to fight.[62]

The fight starts with our hearts, that which matters most of all, the source of everything we do. King Solomon calls our heart the "wellspring of life" (Prov. 4:23 WEB). From this point forward, like vigilant soldiers, we should be on guard. Not an anxious, worried watch but an attentive, eyes-peeled awareness standing sentinel over our hearts.

We do have a formidable opponent, I'll give you that. Satan would love to take us out. But the Holy Spirit–fighter in us can beat him—girls or not.

We tend to forget the Holy Spirit also lives within us. *Within us.* Isn't that amazing! We have God living and dwelling inside us.[63]

I'm also amazed when I see some of the uninvited guests we allow to come in and destroy our homes (our hearts and minds). We simply wouldn't tolerate a negative or destructive roommate barging in our physical home and wrecking it, ruining our prized treasures or putting our family in danger. Yet we allow deceitful lies to worm their way into our minds and hearts as permanent houseguests.

Psalm 147:3 (NIV) tells us that when God heals us (the brokenhearted) he also *binds* up our wounds. According to the original Greek used in this scripture, this binding up is reflective of a pretty intense action by God. After God heals, he actively sews up our wounds in a way that prevents further contamination. He doesn't just kiss our "boo-boos" and send us on our way (although according to my granddaughter, Lacey Jane, that does hold some major healing power).

We have to fight any contamination, keep our "home" safe.

When You've Tried It, and It Doesn't Work

What, then, is the culmination of this following the Shepherd-Jesus? This trusting him for right-thinking and surrendering our need for answers or justice? Of standing ready to fight when he calls us to?

It is the living of a vibrant, abundant life. One lived under the umbrella of unconditional love and acceptance, walking out the path he has planned for us—in spite of any adverse circumstances.

> *Silence, shame, guilt, or any other emotional torment simply cannot rob us of God's love, of his plan for us.*

This following Jesus, it's not only about living rightly or wrongly—though some would insist it is. If my ticket to a forever-life with Jesus was based on even my behavior yesterday, I wouldn't qualify.

We can't do this on our own, this is a supernatural thing—this standing for, walking with, and living for God.[64] It's nothing mystical or super spiritual as some have painted it, but rather a simple dependence.

We do, however, risk a vulnerable courage with our willingness to allow God to change our lives from the inside out.

Brené Brown is an insightful University of Houston research professor who has spent the past decade studying vulnerability, courage, worthiness, and shame. (Yes, there is actually someone who researches these things.) In her research, Brené discovered something about us women: when we see others speak out about their pain, we consider them brave, but if we consider doing it, we tend to feel weak or stupid.

This is exactly what we do, isn't it? Applaud the vulnerability and courage of those women around us who so eloquently share their stories of positive change while we drown in fear at the thought of doing the same.

Brené suggests a commonality in those women who have found their voices, the ones who have reconciled their pain and are now capable and confident problem solvers and encouragers. They were willing to be real, willing to be imperfect. These women risked the healing journey, knowing full well they might be hurt.[65]

This is not a quick fix; I never promised it would be. This is a lifestyle change. Sort of like changing our accent. I'm originally from northern Virginia but was raised in Tennessee. On my lazy days, I have the southern drawl to prove it. And yes, sometimes, as charming as it is, it can be distracting to others.

Did you know accents can be changed? If we expose ourselves to a new accent and practice frequently, we can reduce our native accent. This right–thinking can become our *target accent*, our permanent way of filtering things.

We don't have to be marked by where we've come from.

In Pursuit of Positive Change

"A leader who wants to make a difference must pay a price," Perry Noble once said.[66]

Jesus calls himself the "Good Shepherd." There's a reason. There are a lot of people who want to lead, but he is the only Good one, and the only One willing to lay down his life for the privilege of leading us.

That's a high cost for leadership, a price Jesus paid because he considers the prize worthwhile. You, me, we are the prize, if we follow his lead.

Will we follow his lead? This followership, this is what changes our lives.

By chance, are you one of those women who migrate toward quizzes in magazines? You know, the self-tests? I'll admit it: I am. From determining my "real age," to finding out if I'm a great spouse, to understanding the ten types of humor, I've taken most of them. Meanwhile, I've discovered I tend to be an entrepreneurial, problem-solving, creative type but I've also discovered I don't necessarily know the healthiest cities in America or who custody of the remote control really belongs to.

Indulge me? I've composed a mini self-test of sorts to determine what sort of Shepherd-follower we really are. And like the cool quizzes in those scented glossy magazines, there's only one rule: honesty. Consider these questions as things are right now, not as you wish they were. Your answers will directly impact where you go next.

---

1. Do You (Really) Know Who God Is?

Will you accept God's sovereignty? Some consider it naive to believe in an all-knowing God who can bring purpose to our pain, but I suggest it much more naive not to believe.

Short of heaven, I can't find anywhere God promised us a pain-free zone. But he does have good things in store for us. He promises. And he keeps his promises. Anytime we're tempted to doubt God's hand in the circumstances of our lives, we need to meditate on Psalm 103. Here we are reminded (promised) that God not only forgives our sins, redeems us, saves our lives, crowns us with love and mercy, but that he wraps us in goodness, and "makes everything come out right" (v. 6).

As Chip Ingram writes, "Nothing will enter your life that God does not either decree or allow. And nothing will ever enter your life that, if you are willing to trust in him, he cannot work out for your good. That's what it means to be sovereign."[67]

2. Do You (Really) Know Who You Are?

You will not find your (true) voice until you are free. But because of the price Jesus paid, you are already unequivocally free. That sort of knowledge could give a girl a courage to do amazing things.

We tend to forget that, though. Forget who we really are in Christ.

In Christ we are safe and secure, accepted and significant, chosen by him, complete in him, loved as his children, assured that he works for our good in all circumstances. We have been established, anointed, and sealed by God, appointed to bear fruit. We can approach him with freedom and confidence. We. Are. Free.[68]

In *Abba's Child*, Brennan Manning writes, "Define yourself radically as one beloved by God. This is the true self. Every other identity is illusion."[69]

3. Do You Practice Self-Care?

There is a natural order God designed: fill ourselves up so we can pour into others.

It's easy to get stuck in the shuffle, lost in the lie of daily routine. What an exhausting pull—this need to nurture ourselves while we pour into others. I often fail at self-care. I don't always sleep well, in spite of the countless studies that tell me how important sleep is for us, how it affects our brain, mood, and even sanity. And I don't always say no when I should. I overbook and overextend. As a result, I sometimes overreact; it's hard pouring from an empty jar.

We need to slow down, pay attention to things that drain. My counselor friend Lucille Zimmerman is the author of *Renewed: Finding Your Inner Happy in an Overwhelmed World*. She calls this slowing down "putting ourselves on the list," and I'm learning to do it. I'm practicing more alone time and implementing more play time. I'm praying more—not because I feel I have to, but because I want to. I'm also getting fairly good at establishing boundaries. I still say yes, but I am learning to say no to the things that distract from my true focus and heart—commitments.

Do you love yourself, make yourself a priority, or are you surrendering to the hard taskmaster of stress and anxious "to-dos"?

4. Are You Ready (and Willing) to Let God Change Your Thinking?

Changing the way we think takes time, repetition, and God. While we surely don't have a hand in deciding God's part, or the timing of things, we *can* commit to repeating God's positive principles and his promises.

As we do, we will see these godly affirmations start to shape our everyday lives.

This repetition of thought is no new thing; we tell ourselves stuff all the time. But we get into trouble when the things we tell ourselves turn King-Nebuchadnezzar-ish, when we lace our positive affirmations with an independent pride, when we start thinking, *look what I have done by my mighty power.*[70]

God's Word is our sustenance, the strength to live as he intends us to live. All the love, hope, faith, blessing, joy, strength, peace, and security we will ever need are imbedded in his truths. I'll sure stick those truths to my mirror and say them ten times daily.

Why We Must Guard the Gate

"Jo Ann, you realize it takes two people to argue—right?"

My not-yet-husband offered me simplistic but wise counsel during our dating days—days when an angry ex-husband still sliced into my soul in ways I shouldn't have allowed. Matt saw the numerous times my phone rang and the texts flying back and forth. Accusations. Defenses. Angry words.

At times we're seduced by unending negativity and trials that drain. We expend massive amounts of physical and emotional energy chasing one crisis after another. We battle some intrinsic perpetual motion, some unknown force that keeps us moving, responding—no matter if it's the wrong direction. But if we're willing to stop this mindless motion, we can stop the negative cycle.

One day Matt lovingly confronted me. "Why do you respond? You owe him no explanation. If you stopped talking to him, the arguments would cease—who would he argue with?"

How simple. Ridiculous. And true. Faced with the truth, I could either run in denial, or stop, make the needed changes.

Slowly, my need for sanity resisted my need to defend my reputation. I started letting go. Those were the days before the iPhone, the days Post-it notes wallpapered my Blackberry screen.

Do not answer him.

Matt was right—the arguments soon stopped.

I wish I could say I always experienced that same outcome. That when I heard a critical truth, I responded to it in a healthy manner and experienced a positive life-change. Too often though, I bolted.

Funny how we run from the very things that can change our lives for the better. Life is hard enough; let's not make it any harder. Have you fallen into any of these traps that may be blocking the very life you crave?

1. **Lack of honesty with yourself.** You have to face the truth about some people in your life. If you're in any sort of relationship that hurts, you need to admit it. Call it what it is. If it is an abusive relationship, you need to find help, tell someone—hold the abuser accountable to change. God wants you to walk in the freedom of safe relationship.

2. **Legalistic bondage.** Our relationship with Jesus is a relational connection, an interaction between two people—not a set of rules we follow in order to get what we want in life. The perception of truth as just another rule, another responsibility, is exhausting and an unintended bondage. We have to stay in close proximity with Jesus; lean in so close to him that his very breath warms these cold, hard places while he points us to a truth that sets us free.

3. **Lack of healthy community.** We can't help but be influenced by those with whom we spend our time—it's that whole "birds of a feather" thing. People with the same beliefs and morals tend to group together, so we have to watch who we hang out with. Watch what we read, see, hear. It's crucial to find and maintain healthy relationships.

4. **Stuffing our feelings.** When we mask our emotions, push them inside, they turn to a resentment that makes its way into our daily lives. It's important to process our pain, to be able to say, "I've got this feeling (good or bad) and I'm not quite sure what to do with it."

5. **Losing ourselves when dealing with difficult people and situations.** We can be transported to an unsafe place by a mere tone or action. Be prepared in advance for these moments. Have a game plan in place to refute the Enemy's lies, to replace them with the truth of God's Word, so that we can choose an appropriate response.

You know my thing for those self-tests? True confession: I also love Top Ten lists. So, here's my rundown of the Top 10 Things Not to Do When You're Finding Your Voice:

1. Don't mask or pretend. When we lack confidence in our own voices, we tend to hide or imitate others. Don't trade your real voice for a substitute. Give your voice the room it needs to grow.
2. Don't stuff. Don't attempt to please others over pleasing God.
3. Don't hold a grudge. Learn to forgive from the heart while understanding forgiveness does not mean acceptance.
4. Don't perform. We really don't have to have it together *all* the time.
5. Don't defend. Defense usually only validates any complaints against you.

6. Don't control. Let things go. We have to give up the illusion that we can control anything or anyone in life, other than our own choices. We can't change anyone but ourselves.
7. Don't give in; establish clear limits and boundaries. There are times when enough really is enough.
8. Don't discard your dreams. Find your passion and pursue it.
9. Don't give up on joy. Filter everything through God's truth. Learn what is acceptable according to God's standards for your life; don't surrender your freedom.
10. Don't run or hide. Too often, we don't realize how close we are to finding our true voice. It's time to share that story you're scared to share.

> *"There has never been the slightest doubt in my mind that the God who started this great work in you would keep at it and bring it to a flourishing finish." (Phil 1:6)*

Seeking God

Precious Father,

There are days these words of truth and encouragement don't penetrate my circumstances. They don't soak into my being, alter my personality. They are merely a temporary high with no lasting impact. Sure, I feel great when I'm heart-immersed, but how do I carry this into my ordinary, everyday life? How do I break through to a permanent transformation?

For a long time, I have prayed for total wellness and wholeness. Mental. Spiritual. Emotional. And physical. I crave the peace that such balance promises. I know that's your design for me—how am I missing it?

If we're going to battle, please be my Point Man, standing brave in front of me. Lead me. I am willing and committed to do this, but I'll admit I won't always feel like it. I'm going to need your help.

Help me not to obsess over what others think. When difficult people confront me, help me to be prepared, to know in advance how to respond. Help me to replace any lies with the truth of your Word so that I can choose an appropriate response.

Help me to run full force ahead into what you have for me, not to quit. Keep a picture of my future before me at all times, and help me to focus on it. Meanwhile, train my voice, Lord—help me to practice using it until it becomes second nature.

Invade me with your Spirit. Help me pattern my thoughts after yours. Overtake me with your love that I may courageously walk fully healed and whole, loving you completely with my heart and mind. Most of all Lord, keep this stubborn sheep out of the pit.

Love,

Your daughter (the one who can't do this without you)

THE VOICE STUDIO:

Responding to God's Call to Develop Our Voices

Guarding Our Hearts

1. Why do you think you feel such a need to defend yourself in a disagreement?

2. Are you responding in unhealthy ways to the bait of others? How could you respond to someone's verbal assault from a point of God's truth?

3. How do you process the unfairness of someone hurting you? How do these emotions transfer into your other relationships? Into your life?
4. What does it mean to "guard your heart"? What are some ways you can guard yours?
5. How much time do you spend worrying? List the top three things you most often worry about. Make a commitment that when any of those come to the top of your mind, you will choose to pray instead. Choose to thank God for the work he is doing in the midst rather than worrying what could happen.
6. In what ways do you put others before God, try to please them even over God's known plan?
7. What are some ways you can take better care of your own needs so that you can serve out of an overflow?
8. Finish this sentence: I release control of ____________ to God.
9. What change do you need to make in your life? What blocks you? How might your life be different if you made this change?
10. What would you do with your life if you knew you couldn't fail?

Dare to Be Brave

Uncovering the Courage to Take Risks

Hope has two beautiful daughters. Their names are anger and courage;
anger at the way things are,
and courage to see that they do not remain the way they are.
~Augustine of Hippo

Like some bloody-faced bad guy from a horror movie pulling me into his chest, the heavy arms of overwhelming fear wrapped me tight.

The digital radio on the nightstand glared green: 3:00 A.M.

A fuzzy apprehension gripped my brain while a heaviness crushed my throat. My heart shot out erratic electrical impulses, and I could feel the veins on my neck constricting.

I should run. Escape. Something's out there, or worse, something's in here.

I couldn't move. Or breathe. Or think.

An all-consuming, head-racing thing overpowered me. Like all my sane or positive thoughts had turned against me and were battling to win my brain's control center. I tried to calm myself, rationalize the safety of my locked house and my warm bed, but in true psycho-somatic behavior, right when my pulse slowed I started thinking about how uncomfortable the fear had been, how I might die if the anxious thoughts returned and I drove myself into the depths of sheer panic all over again.

It's maddening when fear creeps in and sucks your mind's will, your very breath.

I hated these times—these companionless nights when my husband was required to travel, the ones where the creaks and groans of an empty house evoked terror in the early morning hours.

Ground yourself, Jo Ann. Distract the fear.

I fought my way through the down comforter over to the nightstand. The faint light from the bathroom offered a path to the switch for the bedroom lamp. *Light—lots of light; that will help.*

I grabbed the small spiral-bound, butterfly-shaped notebook—the one sitting beside my bed for times like this. The day I spotted it in the little boutique, the bright pink and sunny yellow dotting the cover made me smile—drew me in. Tonight, I'm simply drawn to the truth of God's Word that sits, handwritten, on the lined pages inside:

> "Courage! Take heart. The LORD God is here, right here, on his way to put things right. . . . The LORD save you. . . . [At] night [when] I am troubled and upset . . . he keeps me safe. . . . When I was upset and beside myself, you [God] calmed me down and cheered me up."[71]

The truth-distractions conquered my anxiety to a level where I could allow one rational thought through: *I'm not dying—it's only adrenaline.* Focusing on that thought opened up room for another one: *You got through this last time, you can do it again.*

Panic and anxiety attacks—a tool of the Enemy—had walked with me now most of my years. Grew up with me, got married, divorced, and raised my daughter with me. Even stood beside me as I became a Christian, and later, remarried a godly man.

Satan loves for us to be scared senseless, because it's in direct opposition to God's plan. God designed us as women of courage—bold, outspoken women. (Not to say that all women were designed with an extroverted personality, this bold courage simply means a willingness to speak up when God calls us to.)

There's a reason God's pressing anthem is "do not be afraid." He knows me, knows you, and he knows we're going to face knocking-knees situations, but God has a vantage point—he knows how things are going to work out, and he has things under control. That's why he reminds us, over and over, "Don't be afraid. I've got this. Trust me."

What are you most afraid of? I imagine that's the very thing Satan is trying to use against you.

Trusting God takes courage.

I've never been naturally courageous. For years I thought courage was something I should be able to muster up, manufacture on my own. But when God reminds us not to be afraid, he tells us to *take* courage.

To those with an anxious heart, he says "take courage" (Isa. 35:4 NASB). To those in need of healing, "take courage" (Matt. 9:2 NASB). To the hurting women, "take courage" (Matt. 9:22 NASB). To his disciples, "take courage" (Matt. 14:27 NIV). To the distressed and overwhelmed, "take courage" (John 16:33 NASB).

Take. Courage.

The words are not a simple cliché, some pat answer. God gives us what we need, and he commands we take it.

Courage.

His, not ours.

This courage God speaks of is his. When he tells us to "take," he stands before us with arms extended offering the very courage we need. This courage, this truth of his Word, it's ours for the taking.

Everyday Courage Builders That Lead to Our True Voice

King David modeled this courage well. After returning from a victorious battle one day, he discovered his camp had been raided—homes burned to the ground and families taken captive. David's normally supportive crew turned on him, blaming him, ready to take his life.

"David and his men burst out in loud wails—wept and wept until they were exhausted with weeping, but David encouraged himself in the Lord."[72]

Encouraged himself in the Lord, David acted the exact opposite of how he felt. I'm sure he wanted to run; I would if I had angry men with stones in their hands aimed at me. But David had to mentally side-step that, had to look beyond the smoke still lingering in the air, look beyond the barren, burned-to-the-ground village. Instead, he had to *take* courage.

There were three key things David did to activate his faith when this fear attacked.

First, he sought God. "He said to the priest, 'Abiathar, let's ask God what to do.'" Abiathar brought everything he needed to get answers from God *while* David asked the Lord, "Should I go after the people who raided our town?"[73]

It's also worth noting Abiathar's response. When he knew David needed a direct answer from God, Abiathar positioned himself to hear God speak. He "gathered everything he needed" before he sought God. This is that atmosphere of expectancy we've talked about.

When fear chased David, he sought God first, positioning himself to hear from him, fully expecting an answer.

It takes courage to consult God
when we feel like running.

Second, David focused on right–thinking. When things went wrong, he chose to remember both the promises and the faithfulness of God. David had a history with God. Since his young giant-slaying days, David had strengthened himself in God's Word. He believed, trusted, and walked forward in spite of fear, knowing that (just as in the days of Goliath) God was still bigger than anything else.

It takes courage to remember the good of the past with the present breathing down your neck.

Third, David spoke the truth. What did a worn-out-from-crying David say when he was wrongly persecuted? "[Although] I am sad and hurting. . . . The Lord listens to those in need and does not look down on captives. . . . God doesn't walk out on the wretched. . . . Rebuilding the wrecked."[74]

David didn't simply remember the promises of God—he spoke them out loud, reminding both himself and God.

It takes courage to hold to truth when lies blur our vision.

For a long time, I had a serious trust–leak. Because of the abuse I endured at the hands of my father, a pervasive mistrust contaminated all my relationships. If I couldn't trust him, who could I trust? That leak opened the door to attacks of fear and anxiety. It's hard to find peace when your thoughts rage war against you.

Eventually, I learned to speak the truth when panic attacked. I kept those spiral-bound index-card notebooks filled with the promises of Scripture everywhere—my purse, by the bed, the dash of my car. It took some time for the attacks to stop completely, but persistent, godly truths can't help but change you. I asked God for help, I continued to do my part, and he delivered me from my fear. (He still does when he needs to.)

"Don't panic. I'm with you," God says. "There's no need to fear for I'm your God. I'll give you strength. I'll help you. I'll hold you steady, keep a firm grip on you. . . . But take heart! I've conquered the world. . . . You will be secure, for there is hope; you will look around and rest safely. You will lie down without anyone to scare you."[75]

No one to scare me. Now, that's *taking* courage.

The Color of Hope

"Does the carnage not feel sickeningly real?" I asked my friend Angie. "There's nothing like standing in the footsteps of history; it just makes everything come alive."

My sports-minded, golf-loving, not-the-least-interested-in-historical-events friend politely nodded her head.

Her lack of interest couldn't cheapen my experience. I pulled off to the side of the group tour, allowing the tips of my fingers to trace the cracked crevices of archaic stones. Stones that harbored the silent wails of gallant gladiators and wild beasts that thousands of years ago served as mere public entertainment during staged deadly combats.

My feet were planted on the grounds of one of Rome's most famous landmarks, the Colosseum. The atmosphere thick, even now.

For years, I'd dreamed of traveling here. From countless travel brochures, the silhouette of this colossal architecture draped across the sky beckoned me, "Come." But my passionate desire to travel the world had never been honored—for I was afraid of flying. Occasionally, I would fly short three- and four-hour domestic flights out of absolute necessity, but an international flight was a whole different thing.

If I was the pilot it might not have been be so bad, but I had issues with trusting my life to a complete stranger.

I remember the day we made the decision. Angie and I sat at Cheddars, a casual café that we frequented. While wrapping spinach dip around my chip, I looked at Angie and said, "Let's just do it." (I've made a lot of critical life decisions over a good bowl of spinach dip.)

"Do it?" Angie lowered her chip into the fresh bowl of salsa. "Do you want to let me know what you're talking about?"

"Europe—let's schedule it."

Angie, a friend of fifteen years, is a teacher at a private Christian school and was scheduled to go on an educational tour of Europe with her students. For months, we'd tossed around the idea of my tagging along.

"You're serious?" she asked, well aware of my fears. "You do realize that's 4,500 miles away from here, right?"

"Yea, but it's the Roman ruins—let's do it." *My sanity quickly questioned my fleeting moment of courage.* "But not without trip insurance," I said.

Angie smiled, nodding in agreement.

For the next six months I worried almost daily about making that trip. The excitement I should have felt paled to the fears that taunted me. *The plane will crash. You're going to die. Why did you think you could do this?*

One day I sat at my desk in my home office, munching carrots while reading an inspirational blog during a quick break. I stumbled onto the words of author Nancy Guthrie, "God wants to show you what it's like to really live free of an obsession with personal safety. . . . Your fears are robbing you of your dreams. I want you to stop being afraid." Her unexpected words hacked my day; the Europe trip suddenly front and center.

I almost choked on my carrots. *A life free of fear? Impossible.*

Nancy voiced what I had denied, or at least skirted around: I was obsessed with my personal safety. Not a cautious self-aware need for safety, but rather a consuming obsession. I demanded my right to be safe. In control. And I avoided, at all costs, any environment that left me feeling out of control, such as flying in a jet over the Atlantic Ocean at an altitude of thirty thousand feet for ten and a half hours.

My fears *were* robbing me—that made me mad. But anger could only take me so far, surely couldn't cross the ocean for me. I decided to redirect that frustration, turn it into hope.

A focus on Jesus overwhelms the worst of enemies.

Now, more than ever, I was determined to land my feet overseas and mine the rich treasures of international travel. I shifted my fear, refocused it onto Jesus, trading it for a hope that somehow God was going to help me make this trip.

On a day in early October, we boarded that plane for Europe. I had been prayed over, anointed, and even slightly medicated (hey—whatever it takes), determined to overcome my fears.

Now, here I stood. Awestruck. Tucked in a remote corner of the Colosseum among nearly two-thousand-year-old partial ruins. My heart full, my hope fulfilled, in the majestic yet humbled Rome.

The cowering is not my greatest regret
but rather the energy it took to believe the lie.

The rewards of hope were great. As I turned away from the Colosseum, a reminder of God's promises kissed the sky—a double rainbow, elegantly arched overtop the regal ruins. The spectrum colors spoke to me of God's reliable promises. My favorite: "Remember that I commanded you to be strong and brave. Don't be afraid, because the Lord your God will be with you everywhere you go."[76]

Be brave.

Be strong in spite of our feelings—a strength that can only come from being in God's presence. Brother Lawrence, an uncomplicated man who entered a Paris monastery at midlife, has taught me much about "practicing the presence of God."

He writes,

> I keep myself retired with Him [God] in the depth of centre of my soul as much as I can; and while I am so with Him I fear nothing; but the least turning from Him is insupportable.[77]

God promises to go everywhere we go. Even to the ruins of Rome, if that's in his plans.

When Hope Turns to Courage and We Build a Foundation

We women are vulnerable to fear, it's no secret. It's because a woman who loves the Lord and seeks after his heart has a potentially powerful voice, a voice that is a direct extension of God's breath in us. This intimidates Satan, so he tries to silence us in whatever ways he can.

Satan stirs confusion, fear, and death;
but God breathes hope, courage, and life.

For a long time, I've longed to write words of hope that would strengthen others, point them to Jesus. And from the time I dared whisper that dream, I held a book title heart-close: *Faith Not Fear.* (Grace here for my lack of creativity? The whispered dream had not yet been given room to grow, and those simplistic words depicted my heart-message.)

There is another path. We can choose faith over fear, the sort of faith that leads us to a hope God has long intended us to find.

A hope that slipped an Israelite woman named Hannah right into the pages of biblical history.

Nestled about twenty miles north of Jerusalem, in the small village of Shiloh, a heart-broken Hannah sat under the watchful eye of Eli, the priest. She was barren, a cultural disgrace, and she had fallen prey to the criticism of others—the blackness threatening to consume her entirely.

Am I worth anything without a child?

The rivalry. The cruel remarks. The misjudgment of others. The weight of her childlessness overtook her.

Hannah had sacrificed most everything—her relationship with her husband was at odds, her self-care suffering, and her social status a mockery. Embittered in spirit, Hannah made her way to God, pouring out her soul like a flask of costly oil. The aroma of Hannah's sacrifice floated right into the hands of God's goodness and mercy. Here, she was safe.

Safe to vent. Safe to wonder. And safe to strike a deal with God.

"God, if you give me this one thing. If you give me a child—" Hannah stood straight. "I will give him right back to you."

Hannah chased after God's favor. She dared to hope, and that hope brought courage.[78]

Hannah's desires were fulfilled with the birth of Samuel.

Later, she honored her promise, delivering a toddler Samuel to Eli at the temple. The same toddler who grew to be a prophet—a world-changing prophet who appointed David as the greatest king of Israel—while a formerly barren Hannah went on to mother three more sons and two daughters.

Hope-filled, courage-taking faith trumps fear. Every time.

Brené Brown uncovered this same foundational element in women who live a life of purpose: courage. Those with a healthy sense of self-worth have had to learn to take courage. Consider the original Latin definition of the word "courage": *kerr.* It meant "heart".[79] Courage as a heart–gift from God. He knit courage into our inner being from the beginning. It takes courage to heal, to break our silence, to be women who overcome life's hurts and use our stories to make a difference. This courage comes from a place beyond our own creation. And it remains incomplete until we allow God to charge it, to transform it into the force he intended.

We have a rich heritage of women who modeled this heart–courage for us, often in the face of warring emotional battles. These women heard from God, were revitalized and encouraged by his voice, and spoke the individual message God intended them to share.

Women like Mrs. Noah. Can't you imagine her shaking her head as she stepped onto the ark for the first time? "It's been 120 years, Noah, and it still makes no sense; but if you think this is what we're supposed to do, then let's do it." Lonely and in spite of great ridicule, Noah's wife supported her godly husband during those difficult ark-building years.

That's heart–courage.

Or like Esther, the young Jewish girl who was orphaned, reared by her cousin, voiceless in society, but later made queen via a world-wide beauty pageant. Can you imagine what she must have felt as she served a meal to the very man who wanted her and her relatives dead?

What about the lesser-known courageous women—midwives like Shiphrah and Puah who ignored the king's commands to murder any Hebrew boys upon their birth?[80] Women like the prostitute who washed Jesus' feet and laid her sin, fears, and hurts bare before everyone?

That's life-risking, reputation-breaking heart-courage.

Eventually We All Have to Be Brave Women

"Do you have any idea how that makes me feel? Knowing you spend your time dreaming of women who look like *that*?" my friend yelled at her husband. "How am I supposed to compete with that?"

She'd snuck in from work earlier than planned, tiptoed downstairs to surprise her husband with lunch—but was shocked to find him cruising the internet for erotic pictures.

"It's not about you," her husband insisted. "It's about me. These pictures meet a need of mine when you aren't here. It shouldn't bother you that much—they aren't real women. All guys do it."

They'd been here before. Her husband acted indignant at first, then apologized and promised to change. My friend yelled, then cried. They went round after round, a relentless, crazy-making cycle of conversation that exasperated both of them. In hopelessness, they finally dropped the subject—until a few weeks later when she would find he had fallen once again.

What does a woman do, when her white picket fence turns to a silent war with pornography?

Though the Christian counselor assured her it wasn't about her, it was about her husband escaping his own unhealed pain, meeting his needs of worth and control in a way that was readily available to him, my friend still felt she would never measure up.

She'd begged him to stop. Prayed for him to. Willed him to. He had to, because if he didn't, it would confirm what she feared most: *I'm not good enough.*

These are those days of battle we knew would come; those courage-building exercises that life forces on us sometimes. The good news is we've been trained for the fight. We already have the answers and spiritual strength to have some of these hard conversations with ourselves. Will we engage the battle, use what we know?

The Courage to Process Grief

This hard conversation may well require the most courage. When life cuts deep, the groans linger. The sheer loss of something precious overwhelms, chokes, intimidates. We riddle ourselves with despairing thoughts about how we should have done something differently, how this pain will never go away. Then we sink ourselves into activity as quickly as we can—as if we can somehow make the pain subside if we ignore it.

It doesn't work. I wish it did, for then we wouldn't have to risk.

In his mercy, God provided us with a natural, healthy process to reconcile this pain. From an unexpected job loss to the death of a relative, from broken relationships to failing health, every significant loss deserves a period of dedicated grief. Not a frenzied, negatively charged feeling, but a mourning process that honors the loss while it grounds us in a new normal.

Perhaps the "acceptable" period of grief has passed. We've attended the counseling sessions. Completed the workshops. Done the time-consuming beneficial activities. We've waited, we've prayed, and we've even shared the pain with a select few as they suggest we do. But there's still a numbness coiled around our hearts as we try to get on with our lives.

This discontent may be holy—an internal call into deeper issues. The worst thing we can do is pretend nothing is wrong.

God doesn't want us to simply endure life;
he wants us to be free, to live a life of joy.

Remember, healing begins with truth telling.

George Mueller, famous caretaker of over ten thousand orphans during his lifetime, understood the process. After the death of his wife, he was reported to say, "I miss my wife in numberless ways and shall miss her yet more and more; but as a child of God and as a servant of the Lord Jesus, I bow."

It is the bowing that requires the most courage.

The Courage to Persevere

A teenaged Mary was minding her own business, planning her wedding and her future, when an unexpected visit from an angel interrupted her plans. "You, Mary, a virgin, are going to have a Son, and he's going to rule the world."[81]

Imagine the Facebook status that would have generated. "Mom's *never* going to believe this."

Yet, Mary did the very thing God asks us to do: believe him when he says we have nothing to fear. When Mary was afraid, she simply said, "Yes, Lord." No big fanfare, no "what-ifs," "should-haves," or "oh-no-you-didn'ts." Rather, a simple, "Yes, Lord. Let it be."

Oh the things we can learn about courage from the simple, honest faith of a young girl.

The Courage to Speak

"In one of its earliest forms, the word "courage" meant "to speak one's mind by telling all one's heart,"' Brené Brown writes.[82]

Telling all one's heart. Oh the courage that takes, and oh, how Satan knows the impact we will have on this world when we find the freedom to do just that. That's why he does his best to shut us up. (He's really ugly like that, you know.)

Jesus knew in advance Satan would try to silence us, so Jesus gave two very clear directives when he brought healing. One: take courage. Two: go and tell.

When Jesus healed the woman with the issue of blood, he said, "Take courage."[83] And when he asked, "Who touched me," she told everyone within earshot. When Jesus healed the demon-possessed man, he told the man, "Go back home and tell people what God did for you."[84] The man told anyone who would listen.

Not a bad life purpose, huh? *Go forth. Live a life without fear and paralysis. And by the way, tell others.* (While there were times Jesus told some not to tell, that was more of a timing issue; the overall directive is if God has done something in our lives, he wants us to share—to tell.) In the telling, we become what God created us to be—women of freedom, of hope, pointing others to him.

The Courage to Start Over

Remember those dreams we had as uninhibited children? The things we believed we could do before someone convinced us we couldn't? Remember that second chance we thought we would never get?

Are we ready for a do-over—a renewed sense of purpose?

With the circumstances of life pressing in on her, a Hebrew woman named Naomi was ready. The uncertainty of life, the pain of losing a husband, and later two sons, the responsibility of two daughters-in-law who now looked to her for provision and guidance—it was all simply too much. But Naomi was a courageous woman, a woman who fought for right control of her life.

I like Naomi. She was one of those women who understood that life isn't always the "happily ever after" we thought it would be. Defeated, she headed home to Israel to lick her wounds. But God had other plans—plans that included a faithful daughter-in-law, Ruth.

Ruth was another woman of courage, one whose attraction to Naomi's God prompted within her a willingness to be mentored, and eventually led her into a second marriage with a man named Boaz. A rich landowner who restored everything the family had lost and made Ruth the mother of a son named Obed, and made her the great-grandmother of the greatest king of Israel, David.[85] The same David who was ancestor to Jesus, the Hope of the world.

A whole new family. Now that's what I call a divine do-over.

The Courage to Accept God's Sovereignty

We've talked a lot about God's sovereignty and how it rules the healing of our hurts. There is no other way—we have to recognize God's power in this. He saves us from hell, true, but he also saves us from ourselves.

We cannot come to this complete acceptance without first understanding God's character, his love. Yes, he gives us the very breath we breathe. No, he doesn't need help from anyone. And yes, he has the power to step in and do whatever he wants. But he chooses not to sometimes.[86]

That's hard theology when something (or someone) in life wrecks our world, robs us of our hopes and dreams.

Unfortunately, the bad choices of others do affect us. As people reject Jesus, their evil actions influence our world, but God is still faithful. Sovereign and gracious. Merciful and kind. And he isn't out to punish us by "teaching us a lesson."

Remember the sparring twins, Jacob and Esau, from Old Testament times? Just like Jacob, I spent years running from my family history, from never-ending struggles that left me wrestling with God. I fought through countless "this-is-not-fair" moments, questioning the sovereignty of God.

I carried these unresolved hurts into my daily life, my anger thinly veiled in the busyness of parenting and successful career jaunts.

But Jacob modeled for me how to go deeper, how to consider a different perspective for this pain. We're familiar with Jacob's wrestling, but there's another part to the story: the blessing. Jacob wrestled all through the night with God, his hip wrenching right out of socket, but with hip twisted and trapped, numb and unable to move, Jacob still pursued God's best.

"I won't let go without the blessing," Jacob said.[87] *Won't let go without the blessing.* Somehow, this is where we have to land. *Knock my bones right out of joint, mess up my plans, I don't care—without you, God, none of it matters anyway.*

This place of brokenness that drives us to a confrontation with our past and a willingness to move forward, an eagerness to change. This place of God's blessing. This being broken yet being transformed.

God allowed Jacob to "win" that wrestling match, but not without first facing his hurts.

"What is your name?" God asked Jacob.

Who we are shapes how we are with others.

"My name is Jacob," he whispered, stinging at the realization.[88]

Jacob. The name meant swindler. Schemer. And Jacob was living up to his name, manipulating and trying to force God's best.

Who are we—in the innermost part? Like Jacob, the answer might surprise. Our identity directly impacts both our behavior and destiny. In order to move forward into the purpose God has planned, we must come face to face with the person we have become. This person will lead us straight into our intended future if we release her into God's sovereign hands.

What a beautiful bargain:
trade all the lies we believe about ourselves
for the truth of who God says we are.

Consider Jacob's prize. A life transformation. A whole new identity. Not Jacob, but Israel. No longer a man consumed by his struggles, but rather a man now fully aware of his relationship with God, and who he is as an extension of who God is.

Oh, to wrestle with God and prevail. To overcome our past by focusing on what God wants for us instead of what we want.

Like the blind man Jesus healed, Jacob was no longer the same man. Our struggles lead us to a similar encounter, an opportunity to walk away a new person.

If we could fully grasp that a redemptive God,
incredibly creative and powerful,
governs our lives,
that he is sovereign,
how could we not trust him?

Learning to Let God Lead

In a simple camp alongside the Jordan River, a new leader named Joshua shows us that when we put God first things tend to fall into place.

In unfamiliar territory, guiding a historically rebellious nation, Joshua could have buckled to the pressure of others as he led a new generation into the Promised Land. Instead, he chose to trust that God, in his sovereignty, had things under control.

One day, God led Joshua and the Israelites to the Jordan River where he called them to camp out. For three days a very real fear stared them down: how would they get across such mind-blowing waters?

How do *we* confront what seems impossible? The answer for us is the same as it was for the Israelites then.

"Watch for me and then follow me," God said.

God will lead the way.

After those three days, the leaders instructed everyone to watch for the priests to come through carrying the Ark of the Covenant (the Ark represented God's presence); when they saw the Ark, they were to follow it.[89]

Follow God.

Lesson number one: God must always go first. Lesson number two: we have to do our part and God will do the rest—even if "the rest" means something as wild as walling up a river and allowing us to pass on dry ground.

Joshua chose to believe and trust God's promises. God told him to get ready to cross, and Joshua readied his team. When God told him to cross, Joshua had to step into those not-yet-separated waters believing somehow God was going to move.

I've been in the trenches of ministry for a while, and I've been blessed to meet some beautiful women with a heart to change the world for God. Some have big, audacious dreams while some are yet afraid to voice their dreams, but all have the desire to make a difference. Yet we sit, wounded, unable to operate at full capacity.

We can't win the war without fully engaging the enemy, but we can't charge into battle without a plan.

You, and I, and thousands upon thousands of other women, are ready to go to battle for God, but the majority of us are still nursing wounds. Some wounds are gaping, open for all to see, but those aren't necessarily the worst. Worse are the covered wounds, the hidden ones, the emotional ones that are ignored as we soldiers feel obligated to press forward in dedicated service.

But when we're wounded, we're more vulnerable to attack, to defeat. If we hope to win this battle, we need to be emotionally healthy. God wants us healed. If he is continually transforming us into the image of Christ (and he is[90]), then Jesus is the most emotionally whole example we have.

Follow. Him.

Jesus left us an example. Will we follow it?

Why Ugly Can Be Beautiful

Refreshing winds of spring filled my weary bones, the rejuvenating breath I needed. I stepped out from under the wooden beams of the modern covered bridge that emptied into a prayer garden. At Lifeway's Ridgecrest Conference Center, the beautiful Blue Ridge Mountains of western North Carolina served as the perfect backdrop for the solitude I craved. Inches inside the garden, I quickly claimed a bench.

Nesting, I scouted the area.

A warm, rustic, terra cotta urn welcomed me. The fragrance of delicate yellow daffodils beckoned me closer while nectar-grubbing bumble bees foraged some of the unsuspecting blooms nearby. In the early afternoon sun, I delighted in the divinely painted Renaissance-like scene stretched before me.

Then I noticed it—the rock. A big, bulky, stretched-out-to-there rock smack in the middle of my European-inspired respite. The natural formation claimed the landscape from the urn to the flowers, standing proud. Unbelievably ugly yet oddly beautiful, the rock engaged me, refusing to be ignored.

> *Because no matter how much we think otherwise,*
> *there are those ugly things that hold the*
> *greatest potential for beauty.*

Like a silent plea from an old friend, the urn coaxed my eyes back. *Sit with me a moment.* She was time-worn with intersecting hairline cracks and a missing handle, uniquely enhanced by the strain of the years. My gaze fell to the path of daffodils that began at her base. Embanked by laurels, the blossoms blanketed lush grass that formed a unique trail leading to the foot of an outdoor pulpit.

Of all things, a pulpit. The pulpit, existing as early as the eleventh century, was symbolic of the proclamation of the Word of God as the principal focus. A platform from which to speak, a place to share the hope of God's healing power. Daffodils and laurels led me *here*?

In ancient times, the laurel was "symbolic of triumph and fame, especially when it was gained after a long, inner struggle."[91]

A long, inner struggle. A decade of my private war culminating here—at a pulpit surrounded by daffodils. Flowers that symbolize hope, strength, and new beginnings.

Hope, strength, and new beginnings.

My brokenness—those raging rivers that had felt impossible to cross—those were the very things giving me hope and strength for a new beginning. A new beginning that led me to a platform where I could share the Word of God, the hope of God's healing touch.

Disturbingly beautiful isn't it?

Pain and strain as the path to a greater purpose.

God's Healing Words

Dear Silence-Breaker,

You must know you pierce my heart, kindle my compassion, as I watch you battle for the courage to change, to heal. You've been trying to do this on your own, and there's no need.

I am here. I see how much you have suffered. I feel your fears. But you are in my house now, where you are safe. You will recover, and be protected; rest in this peaceful safety as you learn to hope in me. I will use these hard experiences for good—just you wait.

Allow me to stir a supernatural hope within the chambers of your heart. Latch onto this hope, for it breeds courage—heart-courage. This courage will strengthen you to risk—to risk stepping into any lingering grief that has yet been settled, risk focusing on the future that waits, and risk starting over.

Take the risk. Take the courage, my daughter. I will personally go ahead of you in this journey. You will not fail; I will not abandon you. Your job is to control your thoughts, replac-

ing them with mine; my job is to control the world. Let's work together in this.

Yes, you have been broken, but you are strong in me. I will use this; the long inner struggle is great fodder for a hurting world. Trust me in this? This brokenness will become a rich motivation for you to serve rather than hide.

Like Jacob, you will make it to the other side—you will lay claim to, and enter into, the Promised Land. And then you will return to help the others cross over. Fight bravely Princess Warrior.

Love,

Your Redeemer[92]

THE VOICE STUDIO:

Responding to God's Call to Develop Our Voices

Uncovering a Divine Courage That Moves Us Forward

1. Describe a time fear controlled you. In retrospect, what do you think you were really afraid of?
2. When do you feel the most insecure? How do you respond or react during those times? Have others been impacted by your insecurity? If so, in what ways?
3. What have you avoided, for fear it might consume you?
4. How has your "happily ever after" been altered? What would a do-over look like for you?
5. Have you been reluctant to share your story with others? Why?
6. How can we "encourage ourselves in the Lord"? How can we get into God's presence and allow his courage to manifest?

7. How do you suppose we can hold onto God's promises when we face so many obstacles?

8. What are some ways that God has shown up in a big way—times when you thought you wouldn't make it through?

9. What long inner struggle do you think might eventually empty you onto a platform where you can share hope with others?

10. Select three encouraging Scripture verses, ones that inspire you to pursue change. Record these verses and meditate on them each day for the next twenty-one days. Please don't skip this crucial exercise just because it requires an extra step outside of right now—you will see a difference. After twenty-one days, return here to record the results.

The Silent Many

Why God Wants Us to Speak Up for Others

Speak up for the people who have no voice,
for the rights of all the down-and-outers.
~Proverbs 31:8

"It's time for a decision," Mike said. "I think we have to accept that you aren't going to be able to return to work, Jo Ann. We said we would give it a couple more months but if we're candid about this, your health has actually declined."

For over four years, I had worked with Mike and his wife Denise. I was the director of development, managing and raising funds for Mike Jenkins Evangelistic Association, an international ministry that traveled into schools, churches, and prisons. But an incurable and chronic illness was about to change that.

I held the cell phone in silence for a few moments.

How do you act, what do you say,
when you feel nothing?

The smell of the hot buttered rum candle floated through the air. On my couch, I sat propped up with oversized pillows, covered by a light tan throw and surrounded by books. After a routine surgery had left me battling crippling neuropathy and overwhelming fatigue, this had become my daily ritual of relaxation. With Mike still on the phone chattering about trusting in God's best for me (and meaning it), I glanced outside.

Gnarled leaves held tight to the proud branches of the heroic oak standing outside my living room window. A stark winter landscape had long replaced the glory of the autumn foliage in the woods bordering my home. The leathery oak, a barren reflection of its once imposing stature, appeared lifeless.

Lifeless. Much like I felt, battling to regain my health, watching the days pass.

Are you in this, God? How are you working here—or are you? You do realize I'm losing my job? My health insurance? Not to mention that the ministry needs me—who will help them?

About two months before, I sat in this same spot watching falling leaves dot the sky. Brushstrokes of citrus orange and cranberry red had changed my thoughts to warm cider and cocoa, watering my hopes that I would return to work soon.

"We will carry your insurance through the end of the year to help you in the transition," Mike's voice drew me back to the conversation at hand. "I wish there was more we could do."

"Oh, this is not your fault. You, Denise, and the entire board have done more than enough, standing with me, providing for me in incomprehensible ways," I heard myself say. "I'm sorry I've failed you—I was sure I would be able to return to work."

Fall had turned to winter. And the cocoa on the table didn't hold the news I had hoped for. Even the oak, with which I had felt a commonality, seemed to mock me. For all of her scars, for all of her perceived lifelessness, *she* had seen it coming—she was prepared. She would soon rustle again in the wind, trusting her seed and her seasons to a sovereign God.

As summer faded, the oak had undergone a chemical process in preparation for this day, this desolate parchedness. Trees require water to live, but during a harsh winter, water is scarce and the trees are forced to live off stored reserves. In spite of the brutal elements, the oak could adjust—her survival strategy part of a simple, divinely designed cycle.

Stored reserves. If only I had some. If only I, too, had prepared in advance for this dry spell. Instead, I held tight, refused to yield to the natural process, clinging tightly to my gnarledness.

"Will you let go of what was for what could be?" The thought pressed my heart.

When hope runs thin,
it's hard to fathom that greater things wait.
But God promises us the end
is far better than the beginning.

Remember our friend Haggai, the one who encouraged the exiles to re-engage life from a new perspective? The one who stirred up hope for those who had tried before to start over, but failed? God was about to use him once again to stir a forward-focus.

After ending the conversation with Mike, I picked up the burgundy-colored, purse-sized Bible that lay in front of me on the couch. I ran my hand across the open pages I'd been studying.

"[This] is going to end up far better than it started out, a . . . glorious finish: a place in which I [God] will hand out wholeness and holiness."[93] As I read Haggai's words, I felt God speaking through them about my already-lost-my-health, just-lost-my-job situation.

Me and that oak? We did share some pretty important commonalities. We were both planted by God to display his glory, and in the end, both of us survived that long winter season. A few years on the other side of it, I can see how Haggai was right.

That illness that forced me to leave my job? That plunged me into financial uncertainty? That same illness set the stage for times of quiet where I could dig deeper into God's truths. And it allowed me the freedom to launch a freelance writing career where I was privileged to share words of hope with countless women—the very thing I'd longed to do most of my life. The thing that made me feel most alive.

Greater. Things. Wait.

Like fresh buds swelling at the base
of a wintered branch,
a season of hope beckons us.
The time is now. Let go.
Only when you release yesterday
can tomorrow come.

When Seed Spreads Life Everywhere

Courting five decades does funny things to a gal. As the years pass, I'm feeling a little more philosophical and introspective, a little more willing to look inside at the person I've been, the person I am, and the person I'm becoming. I now know I've been too hard on the person I was. If not for her, I would have no story. She taught me much about life—hard things, yes, but some great things, too. One of the most valuable things she taught me was that God wants to use me.

God wants to use me.

The God of no beginning, whose existence will never end, the One who established the world with his wisdom, the God who could, with a flick of his finger, cast off demons—he chooses to use *me* to fulfill a unique purpose in this world.

To think God could somehow take this crazy chaos-driven, mixed up mess of mine and weave it into his perfect plan. A few years back, if you had told me God would use me in the ways he has, I would have questioned your sanity.

How can we influence others,
lead them into lives of freedom from weakness
and fear, lives of purpose,
if we live so far outside of that ourselves?

There is no limit to what God can do with a surrendered heart. It all started with a seed of hope. One little seed. A seed that grew bigger and bigger and bigger, until it became bigger than the circumstance.

Much like another seed a mother once had the opportunity to sow. The thirty-first chapter of Proverbs receives a lot of attention for its description of a worthy woman, but the earlier part of that passage is sometimes overlooked. Cradled at the beginning of Proverbs 31 is a rich vein of wisdom that starts with the heart of a concerned mother for her son.

King Lemuel was the Hebrew king some credit with offering us the virtues of an excellent wife, but I suspect his standards came straight from his mother. Mom had long before given him strong warnings against certain vices that could threaten his freedom: wine and wrong women. But more than that, she pressed her son to focus on the greater priorities of life. "Speak up for the people who have no voice, for the rights of all the down-and-outers. Speak out for justice."[94]

Years later, that beautiful young girl named Esther managed to do just that. Unexpectedly finding herself in a position of influence, she knew it was her chance to speak up when those close to her were threatened, her chance to be a voice for those who had no voice.

While God can and does use us because of our circumstances, sometimes he actually places us in certain circumstances intentionally. *For such a time as this.*

God's answer for the fear that comes from the oppression of others? Speak up. Esther was told, "If you choose to remain silent at this time . . . you and your family will perish."[95] Seems quite the consequence for not speaking out.

There is a divine hope that lies within our hurts.
God uses the broken heart of one
to mend the brokenness of another,
uses me to help you, uses you to help me.
This God-centered pain changes the world,
one woman at a time.

"The imprisoned ones will soon be released. . . . I [God] put my words in your mouth."[96]

This is why I share my story. Open this heart wide, pour out my past vulnerable and red, in the pure hope that something about my life will offer a validity that connects me with you. You now know I've seen pain, and made it through. You know I understand how life can hurt. But you also know I want you free—emotionally whole and living a life of joy. So when I challenge you, you know it is not some evasive response for something I really can't comprehend. It's a genuine desire to see your life changed—to see hope bloom fresh in the dry places.

We've agreed: life is messy sometimes. In this past year alone, a couple I know buried their two-year-old daughter, a single mom was diagnosed with breast cancer, and a high school senior discovered she was pregnant—by her stepfather. On a national level, we've faced extreme weather tragedies, as well as unspeakable crimes and blatant abuse of power.

God doesn't always protect us from pain. (I'm sure he has his reasons—though I won't pretend to understand them.) I hope that doesn't stir doubt, but God simply doesn't fit our image of the genie-of-the-lamp god who grants all our wishes.

Every day I talk to hurting women who feel used up. Spent and discarded. From the wife whose husband refuses to let her voice a simple opinion, to the young girl bought and sold as a sex slave. From the young mom struggling for meaning in life to the grandmother who feels it's too late to matter. From the woman walking through the pain of a husband addicted to pornography to the young girl being abused by a family relative. From the wife who can't maintain an intimate relationship with her husband to the wife who was punched in the face last Saturday night.

There are so many—how could we possibly make a real difference, right? God cares about every single woman, and has a plan for her healing. As Esther discovered, that plan might just include me and you.

Gleaning the Wheat in the Blowing Wind

Legs crossed Indian-style, palms facing upward and resting on each knee, I sat in the middle of my living room floor meditating. Not meditating as in I-practice-yoga-meditating (because I don't), but rather a collapsing-in-the-floor-exhausted-with-too-much-on-my mind posture. (Although, the palms landing upward may well have been a subliminal sign of a surrender that was to come.)

Tears soaked the long hair that clung to my face—hair that hadn't been brushed in forty-eight hours. With Tabitha safely away at her father's for the weekend, I had time to think for once. Too much time.

I called myself a Christian—I wasn't one. I told people I was married, but I had no marriage. Not a real one anyway. I convinced myself I was doing everything I could and what was right, but in so many ways I wasn't.

It all came crashing forward, met me face-to-face right there on the floor—the insecurities and broken heart; the shattered dreams and unmet expectations; the sacrifices, the need for validation and the desire for revenge; the longing to understand and the temptation to quit. Slowly, methodically, I sifted through to see if any good remained, much like separating wheat on a threshing floor.

In ancient times, a threshing floor served as a place for farmers to bring sheaves of grain from the fields to harvest them. The grain was laid out in a high open area, exposed to the wind. Animals, oxen and donkeys were often used to trample the sheaves in order to loosen the grain from the husks, the chaff.

The sheaves were crushed. Threshed. Stripped bare until their nutritional value was all that remained, the chaff pile tossed to the wind.

Without the bearing down, the trampling,
the necessary separation,
we would remain tangled in the bad
with no lasting harvest.

Just like the sheaves, I was stripped bare to the core of who God created me to be, to the real substance within. All those things that had blocked God's best for me over the years poured out here, in my open space between two couches, an area rug, and my outstretched arms.

I'm unsure how long I remained, but it was long enough to finally get things right with God. The quiet surrender that came was much more difficult than the pride-swallowing trek I had made to the front of a church one Sunday morning. That same morning I bought the "all-is-well" message from this encouraging faith-pusher, the message that never fully penetrated my heart.

There's a freedom that comes
when you deliberately stretch your dry,
shriveled places
in front of God,
when you're willing to smooth your pain
in an open area.

I wonder, have you spent any time on the threshing floor? Brought everything forward, allowed the sieve of God's hand to separate what is valuable and to be used for his plans? I understand the pressures and confusion of life have been great, but it's time we loose the real from the counterfeit—the good from the bad—in this open area.[97]

When Story Heals the Wounded Places

The International Storytelling Center lies in the Appalachian hills of Jonesborough, Tennessee—a 235-year-old city proclaimed the "storytelling capital of the world." Each year, thousands descend on this tiny town for the National Storytelling Festival. Attendees from throughout the country come for the festivities and the stories, as well as the healing that comes from gathering together and sharing.

There's something about story that somehow makes our lives better, easier to live. Since the caves of ancient culture, we've used folklore, fairy tales, and personal experience to teach and inspire. Ask a young woman if she has heard the dreadful battles of the soldiers who fought during World War I or Pearl Harbor. If she has, it's because someone shared the story that survived the passing of time.

The redemptive hope tucked inside your untold story,
it dies an unnatural death.
The silent words and the lost hope,
they will haunt you.

Our story of healing has the potential to unlock hopeless hearts, our own experiences serving as a point of reference for those in hard places. As others witness God's transformation in our lives, they want to know more about the Transformer. This is the power of sharing our stories.

Remember the Jordan River? The imposing waters blocking the nation of Israel from God's promise for them? God successfully led Joshua and his people through those waters, but afterwards, he called them to establish a memorial. He had them return to the trouble-spot (the very place they thought they would never endure) to gather twelve stones to mark the occasion.

These twelve stones served as an invitation for a future generation. God called the Israelites to a disarming transparency. He said, "In the future when you are asked, 'What does this mean?' Tell them the story."[98]

He meant the whole story, from the back-breaking bondage to the celebration of freedom—the oppression as much a part of the story as the victory. And God wanted them, their children, their children's children, and all future generations to know that.

The back story of a soul-wounded woman—the history behind it all—is as much a part of our story as the healing. Unless others see and know the *whole* story, how can they see the full mercies of God in us? How can they see the Light without first seeing the darkness?

Those heartrending wedges of emotional pain
that God has healed
—those are the very things that nurture the raw places
nestled inside every woman.

God chose us to live in a self-aware generation that craves real connections with women who are willing to admit their weaknesses. Women want real biblical and practical hope, seeded in truth. They are ready for our voices, our stories. Oh, that our epitaph would read what was said of King David, that we "served God's purpose in [our] own generation, then [we] died."[99]

God's purpose. Our generation. Then we die.

God has a purpose. And now is the time. I pray that by the time you and I arrive at our graves we've lived out that purpose.

Weaving a Tapestry of Hope from Broken Threads

"Where are you, God?

"If I died right now, would it even matter? No one really *knows* me anyway, knows why I've made the choices I have, behaved the way I did over the years. If indeed life has purpose and meaning, what on earth was mine?"

Fifty and with a newly emptied nest, Catherine Darnell's years of confused memories, mental health issues, and nightmares robbed her of hope. "I've lost so much, God. So much wasted time, mistakes, and missed opportunities all wrapped up in this one locked secret."

Born in 1955 at a small private Bible college, Catherine is a survivor of sexual abuse. Her entire life impacted by what took place during the ten formative years she spent isolated from society within a tightly controlled, self-contained, faith-based community.

With an interconnected home life, families and staff lived as a tight-knit family group. No one ventured outside the community for any services, not food or necessary items, and certainly not advice. Boys and girls were kept separate, forced to walk on opposite sides of the walk.

Young Catherine wasn't even allowed public interaction with her own brothers, yet there were those who were granted free access into her home who never should have been there.

It took several years for the pain of abuse to fully surface. As she stood outside her home now, uncertain what the second half of life had in store for her, it was simply too much.

"I'm tired of these masks. I don't even know who I am." Catherine said as she stood in her driveway, glancing skyward. "Oh sure, there is the public Cathie—the picture-perfect one who has everything, the always-put-together one. The one who managed to intimidate the *nice* men but somehow always managed to attract all the wrong and sometimes married men—but who am *I* beneath all that, God?"

It's the real and raw with God
that holds the greatest healing potential.

As a child, a dominating fear of authority figures shadowed everything Catherine did.

"We were led by God to this school," her father had told her.

Led by God? How could I relate to a God who allowed me to be abused? A God who brought us to a place like this—this place that is all God's work, this place of abuse and control. How do you speak out against God's will?

Just before her tenth birthday, Catherine's hopes soared. As the family packed to leave the college, she determined to leave everything behind. And she did manage to suppress almost all the memories, but the lingering low self-worth led her to abuse medications and alcohol. The rejection, negative relationships, and confusion of her teenage years overwhelmed her.

"This is what I deserve, what I'm made for," Catherine told herself. "People are supposed to use me, hurt me."

This is the sort of thing that can happen when a young woman receives the message her value is based on purity, that no one wants her unless she is pure, and her purity was long ago stolen.

Shortly after having that gut-honest conversation with God standing in the lane outside her home, hope sprouted within Catherine's heart. Through an online social networking site, she made contact with other hurting women. Here, these women shared their unique struggles—the pain and fallout of not just sexual abuse but the complex layers of combining that sort of pain with the abuse of spiritual authority. Soon, it became evident these women needed specific support and Catherine formed a private support group.

Over time, this intentional and intimate interaction with other hurting women thawed Catherine's isolation. Today, she is a worldwide advocate, speaking, holding workshops, and mentoring others through their pain.

The story of Catherine's transformation portrays a beautiful healing cycle. As we release the pain—tell the secret and release its poison—we discover we are not alone, we really are okay, and we start to heal. At some point in our healing journey, our blossoming voices unfold a desire to reach out to others who are hurting.

How magnificent when God takes our individual voices and joins them together to become one strong, powerful voice—his army.

There is resilient strength birthed in brokenness.

Those painful places we never wanted to be, those are the places a healing hope is born, a practical hope we can sow into the souls of others.

"Hope wraps survivors in a blanket of trust," Catherine says. "Our seemingly insignificant voices have the power to change not only another individual's life, but to bring change for countless others. Our individual thread of life can now be woven into a beautiful tapestry of hope, of strength."

Because Our Story Isn't Ours Alone

Catherine's story can be difficult for some to hear, especially the faith-based community. When one professes Christianity yet slices apart another's soul, the pain reverberates far and wide. But stories like these need to be told—not for the shock, but rather the recycle value.

Dan Allender, in his book *To Be Told*, refers to this as an opportunity to reveal God through our story. The chance to use both the heartache and the hope for the sake of others.

> Since our stories reveal God, no story is ours alone. All our stories are owned by God and reveal truth; therefore no one has the right to say of his story, "This is too weird, painful, boring, shameful, confusing, or dark; therefore I will bury it." All our stories are meant to be available for the purpose of revealing God and connecting us to one another.[100]

My story (our story) as gift, as benefit to others. A precious offering, unwrapped layer by layer until the real gift is revealed in the middle. This storytelling, it's in our spiritual DNA. Modeled by Jesus long ago as a powerful tool of communication, and used countless times in our own lives to move us to change, God now wants us to do the same with our stories. In God's divine design, when these tales of transformation are shared, that same transforming Power carries into the next listening heart. Ultimately, it isn't about *our* story—it is about the *Author* of our story, the One who brings hope and joy, as well as peace and healing into any heartache. Our brokenness merely creates opportunity for those who hear the story to meet the One behind it all.

This pain that others caused? Use it as motivation to mold a voice against someone else being hurt that way. That's how God redeems pain, turns it to life purpose.

Is there anything more powerful than the story
of a woman
changed through God's healing touch?

To tell our stories, we must first understand them. Not simply how the hurt affected us, but what God has done. How has he worked? Moved? Transformed our lives? What did we learn from the exchange? What does his hand in our stories mean? How has it impacted our lives? How is our relationship with him different? And most of all, what does all this mean to the one with whom we're sharing the story?

I default to my mentor, Katie Brazelton, here—a woman who has taught me much about healing past hurts and moving into God's plan for my life. In a coaching exercise, Katie suggested I explore the possible message God entrusted me to share with others. *What was I most passionate about, and how could I best help people?*

Katie presented this question: "What would you like to tell the world if you knew they would listen?"

Now, I ask you the same. Imagine you're on a rooftop, about to shout out the last thing you will ever be able to say to anyone, the one thing the world will remember you by. Based on your story, your life experiences, and how God has worked or is working, what would you like to say?

Becoming Women of Hope and Influence

It grieves my heart when women are unwilling to examine and surrender their stories, their lives, to God's purposes because they still hurt. Of all people, I respect the delicate balance of a fresh hurt that needs time and God's graceful healing touch, but this *is* how we use our healed voice to help others. This *is* the story "to be told."

There's a difference only we can make. Just ask Moses—the man who felt completely inadequate and begged God to send someone else. That same man ended up serving as a direct voice for God.

God calls us to our own Moses-mission. "I've taken a good, long look at the affliction of my people. . . . I've heard their cries for deliverance; I know all about their pain. And now I have come down to help them, pry them loose from the grip of Egypt."[101]

It's time for us to help others escape this same bondage. No more Moses syndrome. No more "Why me?" or "Send someone else."

God's ready to do the same for us that he did for Moses. He *will* go with us. He *will* tell us what to say. He *will* intervene when necessary. He *will* release others from their bondage as a result of our going. And he *will* bless the journey of those who escape.

God intentionally puts people in our paths, hurting souls walking through something similar, and he wants us to walk alongside them. To admit, yes it was tough, and I wouldn't have chosen to walk through that, but there are lessons I learned and I might be able to help you.

Brené Brown boils it down to this: "The two most powerful words when we struggle: 'me too.'"

Us, too.

We've been there. And now, we can be women of hope for those who are still there. We have been given the unique privilege of recycling our pain, of encouraging others to lift their eyes to a greater purpose.

A quiet-hearted world of hurting women is waiting. Will we speak up for those who can't?

Healing Words

Dear Silence-Breaker,

For years I've watched you run. Scared. Afraid of what I might want from you. Afraid I might be similar to the other authority figures that mistreated you. I don't blame you, or hold it against you; you didn't really know me—how could you possibly trust me?

Like an orphan left deserted in a war-ravaged country, these pitted roads of life have destroyed your trust. Your desolate pilgrimage—the search for peace, joy, and purpose—consuming most of your days. You had no idea who you were, much less to whom you belonged. And your low self-image helped you build those walls that blocked my best for your life.

It's time to break down the walls, time to fully let me in.

Your story is not your own. I have plans for it—for you. Will you use it as the gift I designed it to be, reusing the pain of all you've been through? Will you be a woman of hope?

Please don't allow the redemption I have seated deep within your words, your voice, to die an unnecessary death. Don't let your story go untold.

Just like Moses, if you go where I tell you to go and say what I tell you to say, you will be an extension of my voice, blessing and releasing countless others. I have nothing but good things for you. You will find me faithful as you walk into the new person I have created you to be. You cannot imagine the things we are about to do together.

Love,

The God of Transformation

THE VOICE STUDIO:

Responding to God's Call to Develop Our Voices

Speaking Up for Others

1. How do you feel about your responsibility to speak up for others? Are you willing? Why or why not?

2. What might block you from letting go of the past and pressing into the future God has for you?

3. Consider each season of your life: the person you were, the person you are, the person you are becoming. List two positive things about each of these seasons.

4. What life experiences could be "resumé builders" that might help you advocate for others?

5. What do you think of your story as a gift to others? What impact could you have on others by sharing?

6. Is there a group of women who might share your pain? Who do you know that you might be able to help, to reach out to even now?
7. Whose story has impacted your life? In what ways?
8. What is your "story"? How has God worked in your life? How is he working now? What could this mean to someone else?
9. What are you passionate about? What would you tell the world if you knew they would listen?
10. How can you recycle your pain?

The Anna Outpouring

When Brokenness Motivates Us to Serve

Your past has not come full circle to its complete redemption until you allow Christ to not only diffuse it, but also to use it.
~Beth Moore[102]

"Please sign this." The nurse demanded, offering a pen.

"Sign what?" Karen asked, still groggy from the anesthesia and temporarily battling postoperative amnesia.

And why am I in a recovery room in the hospital?

"It's a release form to authorize disposal of the aborted fetus—the pieces of the baby." The nurse moved the papers closer to her.

Pieces of my baby? What? No one called it a baby through this entire process. Not when I could barely walk down the hall for each appointment. Not when I felt I had no other choice. And certainly not when I undressed for the "procedure" with my head spinning scared, wondering how I got here—hoping everything would all be fixed when I was on the other side. This was supposed to be a procedure. Mere tissue—not a formed baby. What have I done? This has fixed nothing, and ruined even more.

Eighteen-year-old Karen held in her hands the first real proof that a baby—a real live baby—existed.

There are times when a hurting heart
knows no bounds,
when words like innocence and truth
lose their meaning.
Times when secrets breed destruction.

A confused, unwed, pregnant teenager, Karen had spent her early years giving herself away repeatedly in the hopes someone would love her. Fueled by alcohol and drugs, the rejection and isolation simply fed a cycle of emptiness, triggered a consuming numbness that led her here, to a hospital that now wanted to dispose of the "pieces of her baby."

This, this ultimate wrong choice after all the poor choices she had made up to this point, was simply too much. The sharp sadness consumed Karen, drove her to isolation. Drowning in shame, she hibernated for the next six weeks. The grief and pain rooted deep, lasting for years, shaping Karen into a guilt-ridden, insecure woman.

How can I go on? Somebody help me please? God, if you're real, can you help me?

A Clay-on-the-Wheel Woman

A couple months after the abortion, an older woman came into Karen's life—a woman who later became her mentor.

"I'd like to invite you to my house once a week for a Bible study, where a group of girls your age get together and talk."

"Okay, sure." Karen accepted the invitation, only because her friends would be there. But like water for a flower, that Bible study became an essential component of Karen's life change. For the first time in her life, she was opening her Bible. (Oh, how hard it is to grow without healthy roots.)

This healing journey isn't always easy
—making major changes rarely is.
But the person who emerges, the soul who heals,
we want to say "thank you" in advance.

Karen's mentor encouraged her to write through life's hurts, to trace God's healing hand. "I know you're taking the time to write this down, right?"

As Karen drilled down dark thoughts from her internal world, she was forced to choose words that articulated gut-honest feelings (something she'd never done). As a child, her words hadn't mattered to the adults, her voice repeatedly discounted or silenced. But evidence of struggle, celebration, and the puzzle pieces of an abusive and dysfunctional childhood soon found its way to the pages of Karen's journal.

In the process, Karen uncovered an unfamiliar voice—her own.

"At first I used my newfound voice to complain," Karen said. "Then, I would apologize to God. It was good I could see what my attitude was. It held me accountable. I became a spectator of God's transforming power through the process. I could see truth. And I could see lies. I could see wrong-thinking that needed correction. The process helped me to develop a sincere relationship with God.

"As I learned more about the true character of God, and as he showed me more about who I was in him, I started seeing things as he does. I knew I had only two choices: I could either hang onto my insecurities and fears, or I could find a way to forgive and move forward. I chose to forgive. And that created a space for healing within me."

A change of perspective offers a freshness that can change more than our own world. Since Karen allowed God to heal her hurts, she has spent countless hours mentoring others, challenging and encouraging young women while giving them a safe place to grow. She also serves as a women's ministry leader and speaker where she encourages and equips women to invest in future generations.

Hope does a new work, making room
for God's grace to overwhelm our brokenness.

No Better Life Coach than God

"Come here!" Wyn Barratt's mother ("Mum") wildly motioned for ten-year-old Wyn and her sister to follow her to the stairwell.

The ebb and flow of the air raid sirens belted throughout the night. The Anderson shelter in their garden, a homemade shelter built to withstand anything other than a direct hit, had long been flooded. Mum, Wyn, and her sister crouched in their England home seeking safety. Meanwhile, Wyn's father, a disabled WWI veteran, patrolled the streets at night as an air-raid warden.

When the sirens blasted the single, continuous "all-clear" note, Wyn bolted outside to see which of her friends had lived—and which had died. As a tree-climbing, clothes-tearing tomboy too young to comprehend the complexities of war, she was simply excited to mingle among the frenzy.

"Is everyone okay?" "Has anyone seen my sister?" Various voices shot out from the throngs of people pressed up and down the long rows of brick-walled, terraced houses.

"Another day out of school—," Wyn ambled farther down the lane.

With sirens pretty much a daily event, school attendance was rare. Even when she made it there, Wyn's days were spent seeking shelter underneath the desk—far away from the windows. And the afternoons on the way home, those were spent collecting for the Spitfire Fund (money to help build fighter aircraft).

Can you imagine the insecurities seeded in a young girl's heart when school playgrounds are dug up, replaced with bomb shelters? When food and clothes are rationed; gas masks, the latest fashion accessory? And when your mother spends her days at the back gate, wringing her hands, as you race down the narrow back entries keeping close to the high brick walls—trying to outrun the latest air raid siren?

The emotional strain took its toll. Mum landed in a psychiatric hospital while Wyn developed a strong sense of uncertainty and self-doubt. A need for safety shaped her, conditioned her to seek out guarded, more mature relationships.

While Mum modeled great courage, she also modeled sacrifice—having given up her dream of becoming a writer in order to care for the family. As an adult, Wyn followed that example, plugging her own emotions in exchange for a peaceful environment, choosing mundane career tasks below her abilities. A servant by instinct, the simple life suited her until a gnawing sense of discouragement seeped into the later years.

At seventy-nine, Wyn lived a sedentary, enclosed life caring for her invalid husband who had Parkinson's disease. *Again the caretaker.*

"Do I have any gifts worth anything, Lord—or did you simply pass me by in this area?" Wyn asked. "All my other Christian friends are doing so much of value for you, and then there is me."

Despite depressive emotions, Wyn corralled the strength to reach out—that's when I was blessed to meet her.

Wyn and I walked through some personal assessments, soul-penetrating questions that helped uncover her gifts and strengths. After a period of dedicated prayer, Wyn soon discovered a love of writing.

"I slowly set down on paper the things God laid on my heart. It was as if the cholesterol in my spiritual arteries was being removed. With the flow of spiritual thoughts set in motion, God swept me along a blessed river—one where all the bound emotions (eighty years' worth) poured out."

Feelings of unworthiness,
a perceived lack of love,
and a loss of hope
are the whip that drives people into a depressing life
void of purpose.

The release of pent-up emotions landed Wyn on a new journey, much like some of the biblical patriarchs who started their best adventures well into their eighties. Wyn expressed her pain, disappointment, and hopes through poetry; an emotional medium that validated her sentiments. Wyn's low self-image was soon abolished in the presence of her loving Creator, replaced by a newfound confidence in the workroom of God. "It is a wonderful feeling of communion and satisfaction—writing my confessions of failings, my questions, and my search for God. God as my partner; we are a team somehow, and I love that."

There's something about a partnership
with God
that lifts a worried head,
soothes a hurting heart.

"Here was my Creator, telling me, an old lady, that I had a hope and a future. A hope and a future? Something I never thought would apply to me at my time of life." Wyn laughed out loud. "I nearly screamed hysterically when I read the word future. Who ever heard of an eighty-year-old having a future?"

A future, indeed. A musician friend discovered Wyn's poetic talent. He collaborated with her on a poem, added some lyrics, and set it to music. Soon afterward, he debuted her song at a church in Australia. And to cap off this gift of poetic justice, the singer included Wyn's words on his next release.

She did it—Wyn looked for opportunities to use her voice, and God gifted her with a legacy for a future generation. (He's generous that way.)

"Somehow even the sky is bluer and the grass greener now that the barriers have been pulled away from my mind . . . I know now joy."

And then comes the time we are set free
from the lies of self-pity, the bondage of low self-worth.

Experiencing and Sharing the Hope That Changes Lives

When the Virgin Mary discovered she was pregnant, she sought support from Cousin Elizabeth. When the Moabite Ruth faced devastating circumstances, she bonded with her mother-in-law Naomi. The young and beautiful Esther also turned to a relative for wisdom and insight—Cousin Mordecai.

Mentors are often a part of God's plan for our lives. They lovingly model commitment, character, and right choices as they share from their own personal life experiences. I'm thankful for the mentors I've had in my own life, many of whom have become lasting friends. I can't imagine what my "today" would look like without them.

There's one friend in particular that has powerfully influenced me.

My friend understood pain. When she was barely a teenager, she got married, but after a few short years her husband died. And his death left her totally dependent on others.

I can't fathom that. I've been married to Matt now for eight years; if he died, I would just be lost.

But my friend's faith was strong. In spite of immeasurable grief, I watched her make an intentional choice to draw even closer to the Lord. And her reward was this powerful emotional healing that came.

God must have known I would need a mentor like Anna. I well remember the day I met her—tucked into Luke 2:36, she stood with Joseph, Mary, and baby Jesus at the temple. At first, I thought maybe she was this insignificant little old lady, but Luke gave me a whole new perspective as I read his words.

> She was very old. In her youth she had been married for seven years, but her husband died. And now she was eighty-four years old. Night and day she served God in the temple by praying and often going without eating.
>
> At that time Anna came in and praised God. She *spoke* about the child Jesus to *everyone* who hoped for Jerusalem *to be set free.*"[103]

Her name alone tells the story. I love how the Hebrew and Greek languages do that. In biblical times, a person's name carried great weight, holding deep meaning and often determining character or life direction (which might explain the renaming of a few of our patriarchs).

Anna. Her name means grace. *God gave her plenty.* Grace to endure. Grace to trust. Grace to recover. Grace to fulfill her life purpose.

Anna's father was Phanuel, whose name means "face of God." Appropriate when you consider his daughter met Jesus face to face. How Anna must have rejoiced at that fulfilled promise, the face of God shining upon her.

Anna serves as a powerful example of what God can do in the life of an ordinary woman who chooses to use her voice.

Scripture teaches us much about her character. Anna is a woman who refused to be held back by her pain. Instead, she chose to live each day with a holy anticipation. And God honored that.

Anna lived in a culture where widows were often the poorest people in society; but instead of remarrying as other widows might have, she devoted her time to worshipping God and using her story to strengthen the faith of others. Her level of commitment humbles me.

I want to be like Anna. Well, not the skipping meals part, but goodness what a faith. Perhaps you too want to be the type of woman willing to carry your pain and disappointment straight to Jesus, and wait for him *while* you immerse yourself in a purposeful life?

What a difference she makes,
a woman who finds her voice.
A durable difference.

God has truly shown me how the events of my past and the deep hurts I've walked through aren't nearly as important as what he wants to do with my future. And he used Anna, a two-thousand-year-old widow woman to prove it to me.

Living Free from Life's Hurts

Like me, like you, Anna knew heart–pain, she understood loss and dark days, yet she used her silent grief and loneliness to draw closer to the Lord. She became so intimate with God that she recognized Jesus' presence immediately. And at the appointed time, she spoke up, sharing her message with many.

What was her secret? How could Anna possibly focus on God, and others, at a time when the pain of living most likely begged her attention elsewhere?

For a quiet widow woman, Anna made a pretty serious power move. In the midst of deep hurt and painful darkness she made an intentional choice, she chose God's plan. Night and day, we see that she served God in the temple, which means she learned to abide daily in him. She devoted herself to prayer. She trusted and obeyed, believed and depended.

Are we willing to completely rely on God
when nothing else makes sense?

Emotional pain blurs somehow as we serve others. Anna understood the importance of serving. Scripture says she served night and day. I suspect that means she served intentionally and consistently in spite of her circumstances.

Will we open our hearts to the greater benefit
of serving others
—the benefit being our own?

Anna also worshipped long hours, maintaining a thankful heart.

I simply cannot bump into the importance of gratitude without defaulting to a contemporary woman whose vapory, mystical words drive me soul-deep. Ann Voskamp, a thought-provoking, culture-shaping farmer's wife and mother of six from Ontario, Canada, teaches how gratitude often precedes a miracle.

Gratitude. Precedes. A Miracle. That might feel like a hard-to-live-out theology, but it is true: gratitude changes things.

In her best-selling book, *One Thousand Gifts*, Ann says, "When I give thanks for the seemingly microscopic, I make a place for God to grow within me."[104] Ann could have stopped growing at four, when she watched her sister Aimee get tragically killed in an accident. She could have lived out her years focused on the loss, but instead she learned to make room for God by lacing her fears with gratitude.

A miracle came: Ann found joy and an ability to fully live life in spite of excruciating hurts.

Much like Ann, the widow Anna made room for God. She chose a heart-attitude of worship, wonder, and gratitude in spite of her losses.

A grateful mind-set serves as seed for miracles;
in the disappointing places that tear open our souls,
are we making room?

The last (maybe most notable) thing about Anna is that she awakened hope in those who longed to be free. Not only did she speak up when Jesus arrived, but perhaps she watched for additional teaching opportunities—places where she could share her message. The New American Standard Version of Luke 2:36 says she *continued* to speak of Jesus to "all those who were looking."

An encounter with Jesus always connects us with a living God who has a long-term plan. Jesus' arrival at the temple was just the beginning of Anna using her voice. She continued to speak, continued to share the hope.

While Ann Voskamp teaches us that gratitude precedes a miracle, making room for God, the widow Anna teaches us that hope is a foundation, preceding both freedom and redemption.

Hope anticipates. Believes. Takes action. *Amazing things happen when women hope.*

If we hope, if we believe, God's deliverance *will* come; he *will* change lives, change our hearts, and allow us to somehow use all these crazy things we've walked through.

Hope is God's plan to move us forward.
Dare we hope?

Anna proves that the best way to find our own voice is to use it, just as she did. Will we do the same?

Can you imagine what we could do—what ordinary women could do—if we initiated an Anna-outpouring of sorts? If *we* started sharing *our* healing stories with *everyone* who hopes to be set free?

The (Real) Story We Are Called to Share

This breaking the silence, this intentionally applying Scripture, it changes our lives. Enables us to overcome. God has a plan, but we have to hold to that plan. Revelation 12 tells us about Satan being kicked out of heaven and the fallout of that on earth. With a renewed anger toward the woman, Satan stands ready to destroy God's plan, destroy us.

But we learn the very strategy that overcomes these expected attacks. "They triumphed over him by the blood of the Lamb and by the word of their testimony."[105]

Through the sacrifice of Jesus, and the bold word of our voice, we win. That's good news, right? How can we possibly keep quiet about that? Others need to know about this potential for freedom.

This is how we overcome—we apply Scripture, we allow these godly principles to rule our lives and it thwarts the Enemy's attempts. That *overcoming* is the foundation for our story, our testimony. The "word of our testimony" is the *truth* God says about us in his Word.

It is your personal story that makes you relatable.
Not assigning judgment, or pressing blame.
Your story,
wrapped in God,
around his Word,
and what he has done in your life
will safely lead women home.

This testimony we are called to, this is much like standing before a court, offering a record of evidence to support our argument.[106] We *speak* the truth of what we know about Christ: who he is, what he does, the range of his authority against lies and faulty thinking, and of utmost importance, who we are in him.

The truth is so important here that God spells it out for us: *the power to overcome is within the words we speak.* The power to be restored, to change our lives, to live out our purpose in life—*within the words we speak.*

Anna had a purpose, something God set apart for her to do. And through everything, in spite of everything (and dare I suggest, maybe even because of everything) that happened to her, she zeroed in on that life purpose.

Anna was to let people know about Jesus, and she waited for that opportunity to come. Waited year after year after year, without getting sidetracked. This simple woman, living in the midst of a fractured and confusing world, managed to stay true to her calling. And she successfully delivered her God-message. We don't even know what she said—we just know she said it. And what she said impacted generations to come.

As a Silence-Breaker, Anna modeled more than one "power move" we could glean from:

- **She willingly surrendered.** A thoughtful and intentional surrender brought Anna into agreement with God's plan for her life. When we live a surrendered life, God tells us not only where to go, but what to say, and (bonus) he goes with us.[107]

- **She focused on the future, not the past.** Instead of mulling over regrets or walking each day in fear, Anna looked forward—patiently waiting for the freedom that came with Christ's arrival. My granddaughter, Lacey Jane, has tasted this with her recent introduction to Narnia. Regularly she escapes into the movie *The Lion, the Witch, and the Wardrobe*, desperate for Aslan the Lion to come, knowing (at the tender age of four) that it is only "him" who can make everything right again. The same applies to Anna as she prepared for the arrival of Jesus, a time in which Isaiah 40:2 describes our hard times as over and done with.

- **She pursued a rich closeness with the Lord that overpowered her circumstances.** "Intimacy with God" has become a cool catchphrase for many Christians, but it's a sad thing to serve God without knowing his true heart. Anna delved into this intimacy long before there was a trend to name it. When she saw Jesus as a baby, she immediately knew it was him because she had long practiced his presence. An immediate and powerful supernatural connection was established because she not only yearned for, but pursued, an intimate trust, connecting with Jesus long before she saw him.

- **She didn't follow the crowd.** This early in history, the Bible rarely made references to prophetesses. But Anna was obviously ready to do what God told her to do when the time came, fighting stereotypical standards of women at that time. Proving there was more to life than a "comfort-marriage," Anna stood strong in her decision to pursue God at all costs. I imagine she may have withstood gossip, others perhaps even questioning her motives at times. But she remained focused.

- **She refused to allow life's circumstances to dictate her life.** In a day when women had little value, Anna's infectious voice made a difference. She walked in the power of God—doing what he called her to do regardless of social status, current situation, or even age.

In Which We Become the Silence–Breaker

I well remember the call to be like Anna. It felt impossible.

For a long time, I had prayed for a total dependence on the Lord—as a new Christian, I didn't realize the hard path that might require. While

I now live each day totally dependent on him (often in more ways than I'm comfortable with), and while I am thankful for the intimacy we have developed, the journey here was hard-won.

Through shattered dreams, declining health, and bitter disappointments, I felt as if no one understood, or worse, even cared.

My journal pages from those days betray the hopelessness:

> God, I know you are supposed to be everything to me, all that I need, but I'll admit what you already know: you are not. I need others to care what's happening to me. And, I need to know that you care.

It is here, in this dry, pain-scorched place, that God led me to Wintley Phipps. The baritone voice encouraging me to never give up, reminding me that abundant life, while a promise of God, is also a choice I have to make.

"It is in the quiet crucible of your personal private sufferings that your noblest dreams are born, and God's greatest gifts are given in compensation for what you've been through," Wintley said over GodTube, right before singing his one of his signature songs, "It Is Well with My Soul."[108]

A timely word can penetrate
that part of us still in bondage.

As I stood to fold the day's laundry that was spread across the four corners of my bed, Wintley's oxygen-rich hope splashed the depleted chambers of my heart. While I tucked crisp linens into waiting baskets, God pressed four very clear directives onto my hurting heart.

Do not attempt a single day without spiritual nourishment.

Here's that *abiding* principle, the one Anna modeled so beautifully. We must remain in continuous relationship with God, stay "joined to him." If we don't, we're likened to "dry branches that are gathered up and burned in a fire."[109]

Have you pulled away from God recently, are you feeling dry, even now? God's presence is mandatory for us to merely cope with the present day, much less focus on the future. We must remain, abide, in this ongoing state of expectancy—this connectedness with him above all else—or we'll live a miserable always-trying, never-succeeding life.

Recognize and accept that God is the only one who understands.

As much as we long for others to comprehend what we're facing, they can never fully understand. And as much as we long for them to love us unconditionally, they cannot. The love we most desire comes only from God. We have to set those we love free from such unquenchable needs. Their love alone cannot repair the lack of fulfillment or mend the sense of incompleteness we experience—it's not their job. We must release them from this responsibility and forgive them (in advance, sometimes) for their inability to comprehend the depths of our pain.

There is an end in sight.

For those times when life's not working, God always has a provision. A plan. Remember the Israelites' forty years in the desert? God provided for their every need. And right before Jesus entered his ministry, he too entered a hard place. But after forty days of being prodded and tested, angels came and took care of his needs.[110] It is often in these tight spots that we uncover a true appetite for God. In these thin places, we're forced to seek his promises, his protection, his deliverance with a much greater intensity.

Restoration is a journey not unto ourselves.

It isn't a trivial journey, this healing. This restoration, this redemption, is a biblical mandate—a life principle to be walked out, and shared with others. We redeem the hurts of life when we allow them to come full circle, when we pour into the lives of others. With knowledge (freedom) comes power, but also responsibility. A dual identity—the healed becomes a vessel for the Healer.

Anna moved beyond her feelings, overcame her hurts. Despite beyond-uncomfortable circumstances, she focused on God's sovereignty and chased after her life purpose, pursuing her calling under the shelter of a supernaturally intimate relationship with her Savior.

Will we do the same? Rise above our fractured worlds? Allow God to change our way of thinking? Will we move beyond these hurts, refuse to be held down? Will we be difference-makers? Silence-Breakers, like Anna?

Healing Words

Precious Silence-Breaker,

It's time.

For years, you've kept me so small—made the opinions of others much bigger than me. You've walked about in anxious trepidation, running from my best for you, tolerating so much that you don't deserve.

Are you ready to be free? Ready to discover your life purpose? Let the hope rise in your heart—even now. Let me help you become the woman I designed you to be, the woman I envisioned from the beginning when I blew my holy breath into your being.

Partner with me. Open your heart and be willing to serve others. Learn to live from this place of hope, so that you can stir that same hope in others who are seeking wholeness and freedom.

Let's start with your story, your realness. Will you serve as evidence of my love, mercy, grace, and restoration? Will you speak my truth—refusing to allow fear, intimidation, or doubt to sidetrack you?

Release control. Lean back into me, I am here—always will be.

Yes, it's time. Time to uncover your real self, your real voice, and to use it for my glory. Time to be who you really are.

Never again minimize or downplay your value and worth. You will become a brave woman of hope as we do this together—as we shape this Anna outpouring. Do not be afraid any longer. Speak out! Don't be silent.[111]

The choice is yours—I won't leave you if you decide to remain the same, but you will surely miss out on one great adventure. I chose you. Will you choose me?

Love,
The God of Peace

THE VOICE STUDIO:

Responding to God's Call to Develop Our Voices

Connecting Our Passion to God's Plan

1. Do you know the meaning of your name? If not, investigate it. (A simple Google search will produce a number of resources.) How applicable is the meaning of your name to the journey you have experienced so far? How do you see it applying to your journey forward?

2. If God offered you a new name, what name would you ask for? Why?

3. What if God is the only one who will ever understand what you have walked through? Is that okay with you—really okay? Why?

4. How would you describe a life of freedom?

5. How could your life—pain and joy, good and bad—point others to God?

6. What have you felt pressed to do, but haven't done?

7. What do you wish others cared more about?
8. What need can you meet? What would you like to teach the world?
9. How would your life be different if you said "yes" to whatever God asked?
10. How can you be a difference-maker? A Silence–Breaker?

Endnotes

[1] Acts 18:10.

[2] Peter Levine, *Waking the Tiger*, 20.

[3] Jimmy Evans, *Marriage Today* broadcast.

[4] See Genesis 3.

[5] Mary DeMuth, "Opening the Door to Healing," *Marriage Partnership*, accessed January 14, 2013, http://www.todayschristianwoman.com/articles/2008/september/14.38.html.

[6] *Back to the Garden*, Issue #46, Feature, Bill Irwin, used with permission.

[7] Acts 2:44–47.

[8] Larry Crabb, *Connecting* (Nashville: Thomas Nelson, 1997), 13.

[9] Ephesians 4:15–16; Jeremiah 29:11–13; Isaiah 43:19; 66:13; 1Thessalonians 5:23–25.

[10] Mark 5:21–34.

[11] Craig S. Keener, *The IVP Bible Background Commentary, New Testament* (Downers Grove, IL: InterVarsity Press, 1993), 148.

[12] Psalm 11:5.

[13] Donald Miller, Twitter, accessed July 11, 2013, https://twitter.com/donaldmiller/status/308275715156099073.

[14] 1 Samuel 16.

[15] 1 Samuel 16:23.

[16] 1 Samuel 24.

[17] 1 Samuel 24:9–13.

[18] Psalm 119:138; Jeremiah 29:11; Isaiah 35:6.

[19] Darrell Evans, "Trading My Sorrows," ©1998 by Integrity's Hosanna Music.

[20] Mark 5:34 CEV.

[21] Gloria Gaither and William J. Gaither, "Because He Lives," ©1971 by William J. Gaither, Inc.

[22] Matthew 17.

[23] A. W. Tozer, *The Knowledge of the Holy* (New York: Harper & Row, 1961), 9.

[24] "Etymology of the word intimate," accessed January 8, 2013, http://www.myetymology.com/latin/intimatus.html.

[25] Jeremiah 1:7–8 CEV.

[26] 2 Timothy 3:16–17.

[27] Isaiah 55:3; Revelation 3:13.

[28] Hebrews 1:3 ESV.

[29] John 4:1–42, *Reformation Study Bible* NIV.

[30] John 4:9. The concept for this fictionalized piece was taken from a feature by Wayne Jackson, "Jesus and the Samaritan Woman," accessed 1/8/2013, www.ChristianCourier.com/articles/282-jesus-and-the-samaritain-woman.

[31] *Bible Suite*, Meaning of the Greek word, dorea, accessed September 8, 2013, http://biblesuite.com/greek/1431.htm.

[32] Jackson, "Jesus and the Samaritan Woman."

[33] Quote by Alice Wisler in talking about her son.

[34] Alice Wisler, *Getting Out of Bed in the Morning: Reflections of Comfort in Heartache* (Abilene, Tex: Leafwood, 2013).

[35] John 9:1–12.

[36] John 9:3–5.

[37] Romans 8:28.

[38] John 11.

[39] Eugene Patterson, *The Message Remix* (Colorado Springs: NAVPress, 2003), John 11:40.

[40] Mark Buchanan, *The Rest of God* (Nashville: Thomas Nelson, 2007), 210.

[41] Isaiah 43:7.

[42] Romans 12:2.

[43] Dan Allender, *To Be Told* (Colorado Springs: Waterbrook Press, 2005), 210.

[44] Haggai 1:5 NIV.

[45] Haggai 1:2, 4.

[46] Psalm 23 CEV.

[47] Katie Brazelton, *Pathway to Purpose* (Grand Rapids: Zondervan, 2005), 37.

[48] Viktor Frankl, *Man's Search for Meaning* (Boston: Beacon Press, 1959), 65, 66, 113.

[49] Psalm 84.

[50] 2 Corinthians.

[51] 2 Corinthians 9:11.

[52] 1 Kings 19:4.

[53] Numbers 11:11–15.

[54] Jonah 4:3.

[55] Jeremiah 20:9, 14–28.

[56] George Orwell, *Nineteen Eighty-Four*, (London: Martin Secker & Warburg, 1949), 32.

[57] Charles Capps, *God's Creative Power Gift Collection* (England: Harrison House, 2004), 11.

[58] Psalm 139:14; Proverbs 4:23; John 8:31–32; John 10:10 Amplified Bible.

[59] 1 Samuel 16.

[60] John 5.

[61] Psalm 18:34.

[62] Psalm 144:1.

[63] Ezekiel 36:26–27; 2 Corinthians 3:16; John 14:15–21.

[64] Colossians 1:9, 13, 16–17, 19–20.

[65] Brené Brown, "The Power of Vulnerability," *TED 12*, accessed January 8, 2013, http://www.ted.com/talks/brene_brown_on_vulnerability.html.

[66] Perry Noble, *Leadership Podcast*, accessed August 14, 2013, https://itunes.apple.com/us/podcast/perry-noble-leadership-podcast/id350415887.

[67] Chip Ingram, *God: As He Longs for You to See Him* (Ada: Baker Books, 2004), 82.

[68] Ephesians 1:3-8, 3:12; Colossians 2:9–10; Romans 8:28; 2 Corinthians 1:21–22; 2 Samuel 22:47–49; John 8:31-32; 2 Peter 2:9; John 15:16.

[69] Brennan Manning, *Abba's Child: The Cry of the Heart for Intimate Belonging* (Colorado Springs: NavPress, 2009), quoted at http://www.goodreads.com/quotes/230453-define-yourself-radically-as-one-beloved-by-godthis-Is, accessed January 8, 2013.

[70] Daniel 4:28–30 NLT.

[71] Isaiah 35:4; Psalm 55:16, 17 NCV; Psalm 94:19.

[72] 1 Samuel 30:6 *The Message*, JK21.

[73] 1 Samuel 30:7, 8 CEV.

[74] Psalm 69:29, 33 NCV; Psalm 69:33, 35 *The Message*.

[75] Isaiah 41:10; John 16:33; Job 11:17–19 *The Message*, CEB.

[76] Joshua 1:9 NCV.

[77] Brother Lawrence, "Quotes," *goodreads*, http://www.goodreads.com/author/quotes/66573.Brother_Lawrence.

[78] 1 Samuel 1.

[79] Brené Brown, "Courage is a Heart Word," (blog), http://www.brenebrown.com/my-blog/2011/8/8/courage-is-a-heart-word.html.

[80] Exodus 1:15–22.

[81] Luke 1.

[82] Brené Brown, *I Thought It Was Just Me: Women Reclaiming Power and Courage in a Culture of Shame*, quoted at http://www.goodreads.com/quotes/737201-courage-is-a-heart-word-the-root-of-the-word.

[83] Matthew 9.

[84] Luke 8:45–55 ERV (paraphrased).

[85] Ruth 1–4.

[86] Acts 17:24–25 CEV.

[87] Genesis 32:26 (paraphrased).

[88] Genesis 32:27 Amplified Bible.

[89] Joshua 3.

[90] 2 Corinthians 3:16–18.

[91] "Symbolism of Laurel," *House of Names*, accessed January 8, 2013, http://www.houseofnames.com/xq/asp/keyword.laurel/qx/symbolism_details.htm.

[92] Acts 27; 1 Thessalonians 2:2; Hebrews 3:6; Job 11:17–19; Deuteronomy 31:6; Joshua 1:7; 1 Chronicles 19:13.

[93] Haggai 2:9.

[94] Proverbs 31:8–9.

[95] Esther 4:14 (paraphrased).

[96] Isaiah 51:13 (paraphrased).

[97] "Word Study-goren," Strongs Concordance 1637, accessed January 8, 2013, http://lexiconcordance.com/hebrew/1637.html.

[98] Joshua 4 (paraphrased).

[99] Acts 13:36 esv (paraphrased).

[100] Dan Allender, *To Be Told* (Colorado Springs: Waterbrook Press, 2005), 210.

[101] Exodus 3:7–8.

[102] Beth Moore, *So Long Insecurity* (Carol Stream, IL: Tyndale, 2010), 311.

[103] Luke 2:36–38 CEV (emphasis mine).

[104] Ann Voskamp, *One Thousand Gifts: A Dare to Live Fully Right Where You Are*, quoted at http://www.goodreads.com/author/quotes/1890390.Ann_Voskamp, accessed July 31, 2013.

[105] Revelation 12:11 NIV.

[106] Thayer Greek Lexicon

[107] Jeremiah 1:7.

[108] Wintley Phipps, "It Is Well with My Soul," *Bill and Gloria Gaither Live*, Godtube video, posted by bill-and-gloria-gaither, September 3, 2012, accessed January 4, 2013, http://www.godtube.com/watch/?v=FCM21CNU.

[109] John 15:46 CEV.

[110] Matthew 4.

[111] Acts 18:9 NASB, NLT.

Acknowledgments

This crafting of a book, I've learned it takes a team. A tribe, a village, a community, whatever you may choose to call it. But it is this family, these relatives, girlfriends, and talented industry professionals who prime my words and later parachute them into the wind—without them, I would be lost. So it seems foolish for this book to walk into your heart without you knowing those who have loved me through this germination.

My husband, Matt Fore. Outside of Jesus, it is all because of you. Thank you for believing in me, covering me in prayer, and being my unofficial "theology coach." Thank you for giving me the freedom to find my voice, and then encouraging me to share my journey with others.

My mom, Edith Adams. Thank you for those first visits to the library, for nurturing my love of words and story. And thank you, most of all, for doing your best to protect me from life's hurts—your prayers have changed my world.

My beta-readers: Lisa Easterling, Karen Trigg, Lisa Buffaloe, Christine Dupre, and Lynn Arseneau. Thank you for such courage, a willingness to read those (horrible) first drafts. For answering those 911-e-mails with such love and grace (and let's not forget those much-needed critiques and edits that helped refine and better articulate my heart-message). Thank you for sharing my passion to make a difference in the lives of women. More than all that, thank you for being such beautiful friends.

The ministry team of Write Where It Hurts. "Thank-you" is inadequate for the love, prayers, and service you have given me and our online community of women. You amaze me; it has been a joy and honor to walk alongside you. Thank you to one awesome team: Lisa Easterling, Aj Luck, Dana Acruri, Althea Richardson, Laura Hyers, Beth Cranford, Rita Schulte, Lakin Easterling, Gail Austin, Carol Smith, Elizabeth Buhrke, Kayla Watts, and Christine Dupre.

Our blog readers and community of women at WriteWhereItHurts.com. It is you who started this weaving of hope-words to help you find your way. Thank you for allowing me to be a voice for your hurts while I share these stories that somehow stir healing. You—your courage to step into the hard places—you amaze and inspire me.

The WordServe Literary Agency team and agency-mates. Thank you Greg Johnson (and wife, Becky) for being one awesome coach/agent. Thank you both for just being the kind of folks who make a difference in this world. Thank you WordServe Water Cooler mates for so freely sharing your wisdom, inspiration, and encouragement—I often wonder how I ever made it "in," but how blessed I am to glean from such a talented and loving community of authors.

The brave-hearted women whose stories I've shared. What an honor to share your stories; you've faced unfathomable trials with such heroic faith. Your heartfelt words and rich inspiration are like an intricate tapestry, swaddling us in a beautiful comfort, even as they challenge us to walk in freedom.

My friends, Angie Grizzle and Michelle Reagan. The babysitting, the errands, the hot meals, and the massive doses of chocolate—they have carved for you a special place in my heart. Thank you for loving me unconditionally, even at midnight after you have fallen fast asleep and I call with yet another "urgent" need.

My "real-life" family: my daughter, Tabitha James, and grandchildren, Lacey Jane Barry and Nathaniel Cole James. I owe you this—this model of pursuing your dreams alongside this legacy of hope in Jesus. It is this that will carry you when life simply doesn't make sense.

My "online" family: Whether through Facebook, Twitter, LinkedIn, Pinterest, or my blog, you are an integral part of my family. Thank you for your faithful prayers and encouragement. Thank you for the late-night responses to my random research questions. Thank you for believing in me. And thank you for choosing to be a part of my world—what a joy you are.

The Leafwood Publishing Team. Thank you Leonard, for taking a chance on me. Thank you Gary, for catching the vision and championing this book. And thank you Robyn, Duane, Phil, Seth, Ryan, Mary, and Lettie for partnering on this project with me. You guys rock.

Industry veterans. Thank you Cecil Murphey, Eva Marie Everson, Chip MacGregor, Mary DeMuth, Rachelle Gardner, Holley Gerth, and countless others for those initial breaths of encouragement—that I really could do this.

Dear, sweet Jesus. Thank you for hearing every word that someone else rejected, thank you for healing my hurts, and restoring my voice. Thank you for using me, in spite of me.

About the Author

Jo Ann Fore is passionate about women walking in freedom. As an author and certified life coach, she leads women into full, free lives—lives of joy and purpose. While her own story is one of brokenness, it's also a hope-filled story where God's grace and mercy run deep.

With a willingness to step into the hard places, Jo Ann serves that same powerful promise of hope to a woman's heart. She often writes about the tough challenges today's Christian women face—proving how God can use every piece of our lives, no matter how broken.

As the founder of the vibrant virtual community Write Where It Hurts, Jo Ann and her ministry team inspire women with daily doses of hope, encouragement, and practical support.

As an author, Jo Ann is known for her straight talk, powerful biblical insights, and practical hope, as she leads women to:

- Pull down mental traps and strip away their false sense of power.
- Connect within healthy community, even when they've been hurt.
- Tame negative emotions so they can focus on what matters.
- Share the stories they've been hesitant to share.

The "everyday" Jo Ann loves peppermint herbal tea and a great organic salad. She is a nerd with an insatiable appetite for words—an absolute book-freak and perpetual student. When her nose isn't buried in a great book (or three), you can usually find her submerged in her favorite warm-water pool, traveling across the country, or hanging out with her four-year-old granddaughter.

She and comedy-magician husband Matt live in the mountains of Tennessee, where she talks incessantly about her daughter, Tabitha, and grandchildren, Lacey and Nathaniel, to anyone who will listen.

For more information or to personally connect with Jo Ann:

www.WriteWhereItHurts.org

www.JoAnnFore.com